SPAS & HOT TUBS
How To Plan, Install & Enjoy
by A. Cort Sinnes

Contents

Published by HPBooks
a division of Price Stern Sloan, Inc.
360 North La Cienega Boulevard
Los Angeles, CA 90048
ISBN: 0-89586-161-5
Library of Congress Card Number: 82-82987
© 1982 HPBooks, Inc.
Printed in U.S.A.
13   12   11   10   9   8   7

NOTICE: The information in this book is true and complete to the best of our knowledge. All recommendations are made without guarantees on the part of the authors or Price Stern Sloan. The authors and publisher disclaim all liability in connection with the use of this information.

Cover photo by Richard Fish at the home of Mr. and Mrs. William Dorich of Los Angeles.

Left: The setting for this tiled-Gunite spa was carefully planned. Used brick makes an attractive, slip-resistant walking surface around the spa. The overhead screen partially shades the spa during the afternoon. Tall plantings create a natural-looking privacy screen.

Hot-Water Heaven

1

Left: The owner located this hot tub and surrounding deck to give soakers an ocean view. Opposite page: This spa was designed to look like a natural-forest pool. Rocks and plants were arranged to blend into the native environment. Spas, hot tubs and their surroundings should be designed to encourage relaxation.

There's nothing new about the pleasures of soaking in a tub of soothing hot water. For thousands of years, many cultures have appreciated the benefits of a good, hot soak. Even the ancients knew soaking in hot water made them feel good, though they may not have known the actual reasons why.

In recent years, though, spas and hot tubs have been treated as something of a novelty. Families and friends are enjoying the many benefits of soaking. This wouldn't have surprised the people of ancient Greece and Rome. A Japanese family would not think twice about what people in other countries are now discovering—the social and recreational pleasures of hot water.

Today, some people are skeptical about the growing popularity of spas and hot tubs. They see them as another fad—here today, gone tomorrow. Actually, the reverse is true. We're simply rediscovering a pleasure from the past. Ask people who have a spa or hot tub if they would give it up tomorrow. You'll quickly discover that hot-water soaking is here to stay!

Natural hot springs were popular as resorts during the early 1900s. Soaking in their hot mineral waters was thought to cure many diseases.

SPAS AND TUBS— WHAT'S THE DIFFERENCE?

What's the difference between a spa and a hot tub? A *hot tub* is a watertight wooden container designed to hold 300 to 1,000 gallons of water and 1 to 12 people. It may be round or oval, with straight or slanted sides. Most hot tubs have a heater, pump and filter—called *support equipment*—to keep the water hot and clean. Most also have *hydrotherapy jets,* called *hydrojets,* and *air bubblers* to create a bubbly water effect.

A *spa* is operated and used like a hot tub. It also uses similar heating and filtering systems. Spas are made of a variety of materials, such as fiberglass, concrete, a sand-cement mixture called *Gunite,* polyethylene, Rovel or stainless steel. Concrete and Gunite spas usually have a smooth inner lining of plaster. Concrete spas can also have ceramic tile linings. Fiberglass spas have smooth *gelcoat* or *acrylic* linings. See pages 15-18. Spas made from these materials can be molded into almost any shape and come in many colors. Some fiberglass spas are available as portable, self-contained units. See pages 18-19.

WHERE CAN YOU PUT THEM?

Most spas and hot tubs can be installed, inspected and ready to use within a few days. You can put them indoors or out—below ground, partially below ground or completely above ground. You'll find spas and hot tubs on patios, decks and roofs, in family rooms, basements and greenhouses— almost any location conducive to a relaxing soak. See the chapter, "Creating Your Environment," starting on page 31.

The appeal of spas and hot tubs has

Two proven therapeutic benefits of a hot soak are the reduction of stress and the soothing of tired muscles. Massaging action of bubbly water in this tub helps this soaker relax.

spread to colder climates. This has created a trend toward indoor installations. Hot tubs and the portable spas discussed on pages 18-19 are particularly well adapted to indoor use. They're designed to fit through doors and stairways.

HISTORY OF
SPAS AND TUBS

The first modern spas appeared in Southern California hotels during the 1950s. Popular with visitors there, they soon became accessories to swimming pools back home.

As the demand for spas grew, fiberglass became an increasingly popular spa material. Fiberglass spas are less expensive and easier to install than their concrete and Gunite counterparts.

The modern wooden hot tub was born in the 1960s near Santa Barbara, California. For years, local residents had bathed in the natural hot springs of Big Caliente, Montecito and Esalen. Hot-spring baths were a pleasure, but bathers had to leave home to get them.

In a flash of inspiration, one bather built the first hot tub from an old wine barrel and spare plumbing parts. The whole thing was placed near his house.

Early afficionados knew a good idea of this kind must be shared. So within a few years, an entire new industry developed around the original hot-tub concept.

BENEFITS OF SOAKING

According to some medical authorities, a good soak in a spa or hot tub is a form of *preventive medicine*—a means of avoiding illness. Spas and hot tubs offer a drug-free way of reducing stress. They are said to relax muscles, encourage socialization and reduce anxiety.

Spas and hot tubs lend themselves to meditation techniques and relaxation exercises. You can perform yoga and other exercises in a spa or tub. They help relax tight or sore muscles after vigorous physical activities, such as jogging or tennis. But don't take a hot soak *before* doing a strenuous activity. Muscles will be out of tone following hot-water soaking.

Skin-temperature measurements help illustrate the relaxing qualities of hot water. A skin temperature of 86F to 88F (30C to 31C) signals stress. A skin temperature of 93F to 94F (34C

Massaging action of hydrotherapy jets and air bubblers helps relieve tension and anxiety. The perfect way to relax after a hard workday!

to 35C) indicates deep relaxation. A hot soak can reduce tension, which is a contributor to high blood pressure, heart disease, ulcers and other stress-related health problems.

Spas and hot tubs can be beneficial for some people suffering from arthritis, bursitis or other bone and muscle ailments. Hot water increases blood flow through veins and arteries. Joints become more relaxed. This makes limb movement easier and less painful.

Of course, you should consult your doctor before using a spa or hot tub if you have any type of illness.

Poured concrete spas faced with ceramic tile are more expensive than fiberglass spas. Shapes are limited. Special decking adds to the cost.

A basic fiberglass spa like this one costs between $3,500 and $5,000, including installation.

SWIM SPAS

Also called *jet pools* or *swim-in-place pools,* these are a hybrid between a spa and swimming pool, designed with an advantage common to neither. Slightly larger than a conventional spa, they employ powerful jets that make it possible to swim against an artificially created current.

Swim spas are built with the same materials as a conventional spa—either prefabricated fiberglass with an acrylic finish, or concrete (Gunite or Shotcrete). See pages 15-21 for construction details on these materials. Most prefabricated swim spas come as complete units that include the support equipment necessary to filter and heat the water, and power the jets. Most models are designed for in-ground installation though smaller models can be installed above ground with a skirt and steps, similar to other portable spas, or can be built into a deck.

Many prefabricated models are designed to double as a conventional spa. Models are available with several different accessories, including underwater lights, solar covers and border tile. At least one manufacturer offers a swim spa with a removable partition that allows part of the unit to be used as a conventional spa. This reduces the amount of water that has to be

heated for spa use.

Concrete swim spas are usually custom-designed and installed by a pool builder. The main advantage of a custom swim spa is that it can be designed to fit any space and complement surrounding landscape or architecture.

The largest prefabricated models are up to 20 feet long and 10 feet wide. As mentioned, concrete swim spas can be designed any size or shape, though the minimum practical length is about 10 feet, the maximum practical length about 20 feet. Current jets are, or should be, adjustable to vary swimming speeds.

FREQUENTLY ASKED QUESTIONS

Here are some of the questions most frequently asked of spa and hot-tub dealers and service people:

How much will a spa or hot tub cost, including installation?

The average hot tub, including all support equipment, costs between $2,500 and $3,500. Some will cost more or less than this, depending on size, type of wood and special features. Installation costs vary greatly, depending on how and where you want the tub installed, and what improvements you want to make to the immediate surroundings. Contractors who install hot tubs generally charge between $600 and $1,800 for basic installation, not including decking. You can save much of that cost if you install the hot tub yourself.

Acrylic and gelcoat spas cost between $2,500 and $4,000, including support equipment. Professional installation will run between $900 and $2,200.

Concrete spas faced with ceramic tile are considerably more expensive than top-of-the-line gelcoat or acrylic models. Installation costs are about the same.

Custom Gunite spas are the most expensive type. Because they're custom, they also have the widest price range—from $7,000 for a modest one, to $10,000 and up. The price depends on size, location, difficulty of installation and special features ordered. Installation is usually included in the price quoted by the contractor.

On the other end of the scale, portable spas average between $2,000 and $4,500, depending on size and type of equipment included. Installation costs are minimal.

How much does it cost to run a spa or hot tub?

Generally, you can run a spa or hot tub for less than a dollar a day. How much less depends on a number of factors. Among them are local climate, fuel cost, spa insulation, use of covers, size and location of spa or tub, type of heater and heater distance from the spa or tub. These and other costs are discussed on pages 88-91.

Your personal habits—how often you use your tub or spa and how hot you like the water—also influence costs. In terms of comfort, many users say the ideal water temperature is around 100F (38C).

To cut down on heating costs, you can turn off the heat when not using the spa or tub. Because the water volume is small—300 to 1,000 gallons for family-size units—it can be quickly reheated. To cut costs further, you can buy an insulating cover for the spa or tub to help retain heat between uses.

You don't need to heat spas and tubs to enjoy them. They can be used as *cool pools* for a refreshing soak during warm summer months.

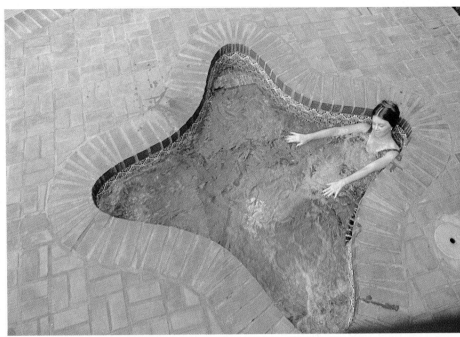

Gunite spas lend themselves to highly customized designs. They're the most expensive of all spas—even a small one like this can easily run $7,000 to $8,000.

Can I install my own spa or hot tub?

Yes, if you have some basic construction and plumbing skills. You'll need a qualified contractor to make electrical and gas hookups. Tools for installing spas and hot tubs are discussed on page 106. Unless you have them, figure tools as part of the installation cost.

Be aware that an *improperly* installed spa or tub, or its equipment, will void the manufacturer's warranty in almost every case. If you want to do it yourself, or want to supervise the subcontracting of work, see pages 25-28.

What's a safe water temperature for soaking?

Generally speaking, 104F (40C) is considered the maximum for adults. Physicians usually recommend a water temperature of 95F to 98F (35C to 36C) for children under 5. Check with your physician before using a tub or spa if you have a heart condition, are pregnant or have any other type of special health condition.

Warning: Drinking alcohol and soaking in hot water don't mix! Their combined effects can cause problems even for the most wary. See page 155 for more details on spa and hot-tub safety.

Kids enjoy spas and tubs, too. Keep an eye on both their activities and the water temperature.

Buying a Spa or Hot Tub

2

The spa or hot-tub buyer has many decisions to make before enjoying a good soak.

The first decision is what type of unit to buy. Unless you've already made up your mind about the unit you want, consider all the options while you're still in the planning stages.

WHAT ARE YOUR CHOICES?

Spas and hot tubs are used for the same purposes: *hydrotherapy* and *relaxation.* But there are significant differences between spas and tubs—even between kinds of spas. Consider these differences before you buy. The next few pages briefly describe and compare each kind of spa or tub. More complete information on what to look for in individual units starts on page 15. Support equipment for spas and tubs is discussed on pages 75-101.

SPAS

The most popular spas are molded fiberglass units with an interior finish of acrylic plastic. In this respect they're like a large bathtub or a small, one-piece swimming pool. Most fiberglass spas are located outdoors, but can be put indoors as well. These lightweight shells are commonly sunk below ground. With proper support, you can install them partially or completely above ground level. Detailed information on fiberglass spas starts on page 15.

Some spa manufacturers offer a stainless-steel model shaped like a hot tub. Durability, cleanliness and minimum maintenance are its hallmarks.

Concrete Spas—Most concrete spas built today are either of *Gunite* or *Shotcrete* construction. In both types, concrete is pneumatically applied by machine over a network of tied steel reinforcing bars (rebar.) Gunite is an

Left: Buying a spa or hot tub involves a number of decisions—choosing a reliable dealer is one of the most important.

Fiberglass spas can be installed indoors or out. Outdoors, they fit into practically any landscape scheme.

almost-dry mixture of hydrated cement and sand, shot from a nozzle at high pressure. Shotcrete construction is almost identical, except Shotcrete is premixed and pumped wet to the spa site. Shotcrete and Gunite construction is further described on pages 19-21.

Poured-concrete spas are less common, except in a areas where Shotcrete and Gunite aren't readily available. Poured-concrete spas require building wooden forms, so shapes may be more limited than Gunite or Shotcrete spas. Still, they may be more economically feasible if this is the standard construction practice where you live.

Concrete spas are often attached to

Freedom of form is the hallmark of Gunite spas. A facing of small mosaic tiles easily conforms to the irregular contours of this spa.

Poured-concrete spas are usually square or rectangular in shape. Wooden forms used to pour concrete limit spa shape to flat, angular surfaces.

Intricate mosaic pattern on this spa demonstrates the versatility of ceramic tile.

Who says you can't take your spa with you? Portable spas like this one are perfect for people expecting to move frequently.

A narrow channel connects this spa to the pool. This spa and pool use the same filtration and heating system.

Some manufacturers of fiberglass swimming pools also make matching spas.

swimming pools. The spa's interior surface usually has a smooth plaster finish. Most have a band of ceramic tile rimming the spa at the waterline to make cleaning easier.

Tile Spas—Some concrete spas have interiors completely covered with ceramic tile. These spas look especially good indoors. You can coordinate them with tile floors, counters, showers and tub surrounds. At least one company makes a prefab fiberglass spa with a ceramic-tile interior. See top right photo on facing page.

Portable Spas—These spas consist of a molded fiberglass spa, heater, pump, filter, hydrojets and/or bubbler and skirt. All that's required to install most portable spas is an acceptable location, an electrical outlet and a nearby source of water. For information on portable spas, see pages 18-19.

Spas Attached To Swimming Pools—Many people find a cool dip in the swimming pool a refreshing way to end a hot soak in the spa. If the spa is attached to a pool, both spa and pool can use the same filtration and heating system. Depending on personal preference and use requirements, a separate filtration system may be used.

It's easier to design a spa as part of a new pool. Or, you can readily add one to an existing pool with good results. You can use a fiberglass, Gunite or concrete spa for the addition. You'll find more examples of spas attached to pools on pages 68-69.

HOT TUBS

The original hot tubs were recycled water or wine barrels. *Hot tub* always refers to a large, watertight, wooden tub. Tubs can be redwood, teak, mahogany, cedar, cypress, oak or other suitable wood. For comparisons of these woods, see pages 21-23. Tub size varies dramatically—from 2-1/2 feet to 5 feet deep and from 3-1/2 feet to over 12 feet in diameter. Popular family-size tubs are 5 to 6 feet in diameter and 4 feet deep.

A recent innovation in hot tubs is the *spa-tub*. This hybrid unit is a wooden tub with a smooth vinyl liner. It offers the rustic beauty of a hot tub with the colors and clean interior lines of a fiberglass spa.

One manufacturer's spa-tub has molded acrylic seats. These and the rest of the tub interior are covered with an insulation material. The insulated interior is then covered with a flexible vinyl liner.

There are several advantages to a spa-tub. It's easier to clean than an ordinary wood tub. The insulation prevents heat loss and provides a cushioned interior.

Wooden tubs may leak for a few days after being filled with water. A spa-tub won't. Spa-tubs are now available from several hot-tub manufacturers.

POINTS TO CONSIDER

Spas and hot tubs come in many styles. The difference between them lies mainly in aesthetics.

Proponents of hot tubs like the natural quality of wood. They feel it blends in well with an outdoor setting. Gunite and concrete spas can have almost any look—from a classic Roman bath to a natural hot spring.

Acrylic and gelcoat spas may be less natural looking, but the choice of designs, shapes, sizes and colors is great. This versatility makes them a useful element in designing both indoor and outdoor spaces. They're also easier to clean than wooden tubs and concrete or Gunite spas.

You can generally buy hot tubs in smaller sizes to fit tight spaces. In a tub, soakers sit upright on a wooden bench. Spas usually have molded seats. Some have molded lounges for reclining.

Chemical maintenance and heating costs are roughly the same for spas and hot tubs, although some chemi-

Fiberglass spa shells can be molded into practically any shape desired. This one is covered with a durable acrylic surface.

cals shouldn't be used in fiberglass spas with a gelcoat surface. Complete details on chemical maintenance start on page 137.

Consider portability. Many hot tubs are placed on a deck or patio. Because they're usually not sunk into the ground, they *are* portable, in a sense. If you decide to move, a hot tub can be dismantled, but it's not an easy job. The portable spas mentioned on pages 18-19 are perhaps the easiest to move. An in-ground spa is a permanent improvement to your property.

Heat loss is also a consideration. Wood is a better insulator than molded fiberglass, concrete or Gunite. Studies have shown that water in an above-ground redwood hot tub with an insulating cover will drop only about 10F (6C) in 24 hours at an ambient temperature of approximately 55F (15C). An uninsulated, partially above-ground fiberglass spa can lose more than twice that amount of heat. Most fiberglass spas come with urethane foam insulation. Concrete and Gunite spas are prone to heat loss due to the heat-absorbing properties of these materials.

Only personal preference determines whether the differences between spas and hot tubs are benefits or drawbacks.

JUDGING QUALITY

The most important consideration for the buyer is *quality*—quality of the unit and quality of installation. When you shop for a spa or tub, you'll find that many units look almost identical. Many buyers choose models based on appearance and the salesperson's word concerning construction.

The next four pages describe how spas and hot tubs are made, what they're made of and what to look for in terms of quality. This behind-the-scenes look will show you what's *under the surface* of the product you're buying. It will also help you choose the best unit for your needs.

FIBERGLASS SPAS

Fiberglass spas are molded from multiple layers of fiberglass covered with a resilient, non-porous surface of acrylic or gelcoat. This combination gives strong, watertight, one-piece construction. These spas come in many shapes and colors.

Unfortunately, a misconception about spa types has persisted for a number of years. People frequently ask: "Which is better, fiberglass or acrylic?" In truth, the acrylic spa is a fiberglass shell with a top surface of solid, molded acrylic. What many refer to as a fiberglass spa is one with a gelcoat surface.

Most pool maintenance companies will tell you fiberglass spas—acrylic or gelcoat—are easier to maintain than wooden tubs and concrete or Gunite spas. The non-porous surface makes thorough cleaning a simple process. Leakage is not a concern.

Following is a detailed description of acrylic and gelcoat surfaces—what they are, how they're made, and the relative pros and cons of each.

GELCOAT

Gelcoat is a colored polyester-resin material. Applied in liquid form, it hardens to a smooth, durable surface. It's long been a standard surface put over molded-fiberglass products, including pools, spas and boats.

Almost everyone agrees that gelcoat compares favorably to acrylic as long as the spa is properly made and well maintained. Most gelcoat spas need resurfacing after about five years.

Gelcoat spas are slightly less expensive than acrylic ones. But gelcoat is more susceptible than acrylic to the sun's ultraviolet and infrared rays and to chemicals. Colors fade under these conditions. Gelcoat requires more routine maintenance and has a duller appearance.

For maximum longevity and good looks on a gelcoat surface, apply a waxlike conditioner called *aminofunctional fluid* every three months. See page 151. Surface repairs are easily made from readily available materials. See pages 152-153.

Manufacturing Processes—There are two basic processes used in the manufacture of gelcoat-fiberglass spas. The *chopper-gun spray-up process* accounts for about 95% of all spa manufacturing. The *hand lay-up process* accounts for the other 5%.

The more popular chopper-gun process involves several steps:

First, a thin layer of gelcoat is sprayed onto the mold. Next, the chopper-gun cuts a continuous fiberglass strand into 1-inch pieces. These glass fibers are mixed with resin and a third substance, MEKP—*methyl ethyl ketone peroxide.* MEKP acts as a

The first step in thermoforming an acrylic spa shell is to heat an acrylic sheet until it becomes flexible. Note how the heated sheet is starting to sag as it becomes soft.

catalyst to begin the heat-hardening process. The fibers, resin and MEKP are sprayed onto the gelcoat shell by the chopper-gun.

As the mixture is sprayed on, the glass fibers disperse through the resin, reinforcing it. The resin, in turn, acts as a forming agent to hold the two together. As the resin and glass unite, a chemical reaction occurs, causing the resin to harden. This forms a thin, hard shell.

When hardened, the shell is fitted with air channels for bubbles and given a second coat of the fiber-resin mixture. Finally, the shell is cured, pulled from the mold and trimmed.

In the hand lay-up process, the gelcoat is sprayed onto the mold. A sheet of woven fiberglass fabric is then laid by hand over the wet gelcoat. Resin is brushed or sprayed over the fabric, saturating it. This method ensures more even distribution of fiberglass than does the chopper-gun process.

ACRYLIC

Acrylic is the most commonly used surface in spa manufacturing. Acrylic is *thermoplastic*. This means it can be *softened and formed by heating.*

An acrylic surface maintains gloss and color indefinitely. It's more durable than gelcoat and easier to maintain. The surface is less susceptible to scratches, though repair requires a special kit that must be ordered from the spa manufacturer. See page 153. Repairs to simulated-marble acrylic surfaces are generally easier to hide than solid-color ones.

Manufacturing Processes—There are three methods of manufacturing acrylic sheets for spas. They are *continuous-cast acrylic, high-impact extruded acrylic* and *cell-cast acrylic.*

Continuous-Cast Acrylic—Liquid acrylic is poured into a continuous-cast molding machine. Two moving belts of highly polished stainless steel carry a thin layer of the liquid through

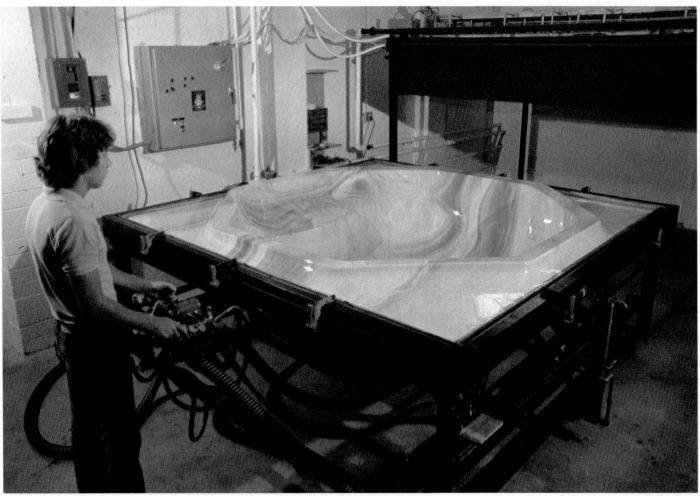

Once the acrylic sheet is heated to the proper temperature, it is placed over the spa mold and sucked into it by vacuum pressure. The operator at left controls the speed at which the sheet is thermoformed.

an oven. When the belts separate, the result is a cooled sheet of acrylic.

Acrylic is colored during the casting process, not just on the surface.

High-Impact Extruded Acrylic— These sheets are made from acrylic pellets. An operator puts pellets in a machine called an *extruder*. The extruder melts the material and runs it through a *sheet die*—two pieces of steel with adjustments for uniform thickness. The acrylic sheet is polished, cooled and cut to length or rolled up.

Cell-Cast Acrylic—Liquid acrylic is poured between two sheets of plate glass. The acrylic is then *polymerized* —a chemical reaction that links molecules—with heat to harden it.

Acrylic sheets range in thickness from 1/30,000 inch to 1/4 inch. Surfaces can be smooth or textured, with a mat or glossy finish. After the sheets are made, they're *thermoformed* into the shape of a spa. In the thermoforming process, the sheet is heated until it

becomes flexible. It's then forced into a mold, cooled and removed. The formed sheet looks like a spa but lacks strength. It's made rigid with a fiberglass-resin backing. Some manufacturers also add insulating foam to the backing.

Making Acrylic Shells Rigid—There are four methods to make acrylic shells rigid with fiberglass: *spray-up, hand lay-up, vacuum-bag molding* and *comoforming.*

Spray-up is spraying a fiberglass-resin mixture on the acrylic shell with a chopper-gun. The mixture is rolled down with a special grooved roller to compact the fibers and remove trapped air. The material then hardens at room temperature.

Hand lay-up is the application of woven fiberglass fabric on the shell by hand. Then the resin is sprayed on, followed by hand rolling.

Vacuum-bag molding can be used with spray-up or hand lay-up. After resin and glass are placed over the

In the spray-up process, fiberglass is sprayed onto the hardened acrylic shell with a chopper gun. Here, the shell has been given one coat of fiberglass and the air channels have been positioned. The operator is now spraying the final coat of fiberglass over the channels.

acrylic shell, clear-plastic film is put over the complete lay-up. It is sealed around the edge, and drawn down tightly by a vacuum. This eliminates the need for roll-out.

Comoforming is a low-pressure, cold-molding process. A matched set of molds squeezes resin and fiberglass fabric to the desired shape and cures the resin quickly, using low heat.

Fiberglass backing is applied to the shell, usually in two 1/8-inch coats.

The final coat is applied only after the first has dried completely. When the final coat dries, the shell is pressure-tested for airtightness. Finally, a 1/2-inch or thicker layer of polyure-thane foam insulation is applied to the underside of the shell to reduce heat loss while the spa is filled with water.

Generally, thicker fiberglass shells and acrylic or gelcoat surfaces make sturdier spas. Well-insulated shells mean less heat loss. Uniform shell thickness around edges indicates the shell was properly molded.

Check the shell exterior for reinforcing ribs around seats and plumbing outlets—good quality spas have these. Inspect the interior surface for scratches, pockmarks and other blemishes—inferior spas have these.

PORTABLE SPAS

The electrical, heating, filtration and pump equipment is all contained within the spa. It comes complete with a skirting of wood or other attractive material.

Although these spas can be used outdoors, most manufacturers have made it simple to install them indoors. Their size is limited to allow passage through a standard doorway. Once in place, you simply fill the spa with water, plug it into a nearby electrical outlet and wait for the water to heat.

Most units operate on 110-volt,

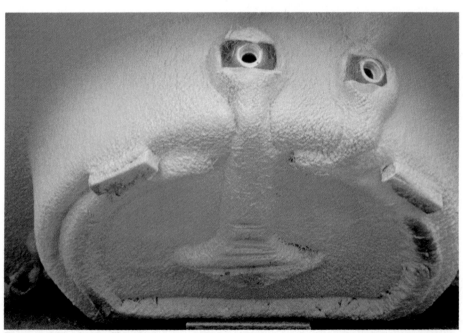

The outside of this fiberglass spa shell has been coated with polyurethane insulation. Thicker insulation means less heat loss through spa walls.

20-amp circuits. The outlet you use must be connected to a circuit of the same, or slightly higher, amperage as required by the spa. Use a *grounded* outlet only. Grounded outlets have three wires attached to the recepticle. The ground is usually a green or bare copper wire. The circuit should also be protected by a ground-fault circuit-interrupter, or GFCI, breaker. If you are not absolutely sure the outlet meets these requirements, have it inspected by a licensed electrician.

Portable spas offer a variety of heating systems, from 110-volt, 1.5-KW heating systems for the smallest spas up to 220-volt, 6-KW systems for the largest. Gas-fired heating systems are also available. The size of the heater you choose will depend on the size of the spa, whether it's used indoors or outdoors, outdoor temperatures and how quickly you want the water heated. A 1.5 kilowatt heater takes considerable time to heat water—about 5 hours to raise the water temperature of a 150-gallon spa 20 degrees. A heater of this size is not recommended for spas with over a 200-gallon capacity. For more on sizing heaters, see pages 88-89. Experienced dealers can also recommend an appropriate size heater for the spa you choose.

Some 220-volt portable spa systems take less time to heat the water. You can only put them in locations with 220-volt service.

The ideas behind portable spas are sound ones. They're great for renters and people who move often. Installation is simple. Their prices are generally competitive with component kits.

Today, a portable spa can be purchased in almost any size and shape. Advantages of portables are reduced cost, the ability to move the unit to another location or even sell it. Also, it remains personal property so it is not taxed as real property or a home improvement. Because it is personal property, larger medical deductions are often allowed if the spa is prescribed by a physician for physical therapy.

Most portable spas are equipped with a combination of air blower and hydrojets to agitate the water. When the system is on with the air blower running, the water cools down considerably, maintaining its maximum temperature for only 15-20 minutes. However, the air blower is usually

The only requirement for locating a portable spa is a nearby source of electricity. One advantage is that the spa can be moved indoors during the cold season.

running only for a few minutes during normal spa use so the water temperature does not drop significantly.

Most portables are designed to fit through a standard doorway. This can be both an asset and a drawback. The most obvious drawback is the maximum water depth of approximately 24 to 26 inches. However, many manufacturers have overcome the depth problem with novel seating designs.

Another thing to consider is the ease in which the spa can be moved from one location to another. How heavy is the unit? Are special tools or complicated procedures required to dismantle and set up the unit each time it's moved? How long does the procedure take? This can be an important consideration if you plan on moving the spa around, even if only indoors for the winter each year. Also, mechanical components should be easily accessible for servicing or repair.

CONCRETE SPAS

There are two basic methods of building a concrete spa. The most widely used method employs pneumatically applied concrete, called *Gunite* or *Shotcrete*. The other method uses conventional poured concrete. Many concrete spas are built in con-

Spraying Gunite

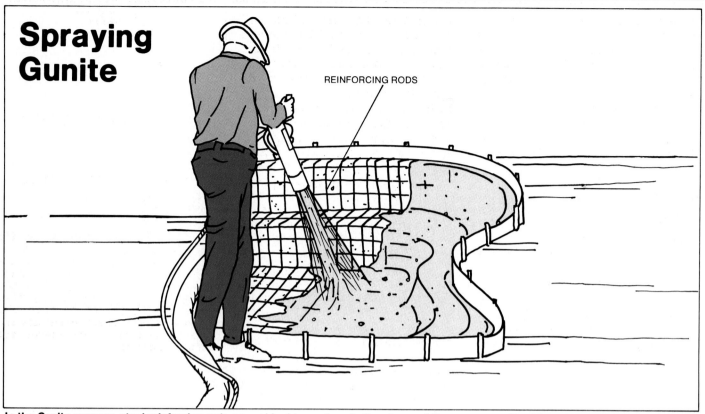

REINFORCING RODS

In the Gunite process, steel reinforcing rods are webbed to conform to the shape of the spa excavation. Then the operator sprays Gunite over the webbing.

junction with concrete swimming pools.

Gunite and Shotcrete are the most common concrete spas built today. Poured-concrete spas are less common, but are occasionally built in areas where Gunite and Shotcrete equipment isn't available.

Gunite and Shotcrete—Strength and flexibility are the primary assets of Gunite or Shotcrete construction. Gunite spas are formed by shooting an almost-dry mixture of hydrated cement and sand from a nozzle to cover a network of tied steel reinforcing bars (rebar). This forms a durable, seamless, one-piece shell. Shotcrete construction is almost identical, except Shotcrete is premixed and pumped wet to the spa site.

After the spa site is excavated, the plumbing is roughed in. Rebar is webbed into the hole. Different-sized rods are used for different parts of the spa. A flexible wooden form wraps around the perimeter like a hoop to form the edges of the spa.

After the framework is complete, Gunite or Shotcrete is applied. After

it is in place, electrical wiring and gas hookups are installed. Then the spa may be tiled around the water line to make cleaning easier. Finally, a pre-coat of plaster is applied, followed by a second, finishing coat.

There are several advantages to Gunite and Shotcrete spas. They can be created in almost any custom shape, often to complement the design of an adjoining swimming pool.

Gunite and Shotcrete construction has some disadvantages. It requires skilled workmanship and an experienced builder. The Gunite or Shotcrete must be sprayed evenly to assure uniform wall thickness of the spa shell. A custom Gunite or Shotcrete spa is usually more expensive than other types.

The plastered surface is rougher and more porous than other spa surfaces. As a result, a concrete spa may be harder to keep clean. Algae formation is also a problem. Until the plaster has cured and the spa is free of plaster dust and other debris, it will be harder to chemically balance the water.

Poured Concrete—This system is seldom used because it involves costly labor and complex forms, and it limits design options. Poured-concrete spas are usually geometric in shape. They can be built in curved shapes, but this requires expensive form work. Heavier equipment is needed to bring in materials. Access usually has to be provided for heavy transit-mix trucks.

A poured-concrete spa is an alternative to Gunite or Shotcrete in areas where these methods are not available. But in many of these areas, poured-concrete spas have been mostly replaced by the more popular fiberglass spas.

Once the wooden forms are built and the plumbing outlets installed, rebar is set, and the concrete is poured. When the concrete hardens, forms are removed and the spa is given a plaster finish.

WOODEN TUBS

Because hot tubs are made of wood, they have characteristics that set them apart from spas.

Hot-tub builders still employ old-world *coopering,* or barrel-building techniques in tub construction. The tub sides consist of bevel-cut, vertical staves, grooved to fit snugly around the tub bottom. Hoops or flat bands lock the staves together. When the tub is filled with water, the wood expands, making all joints watertight.

A small amount of leakage, called *weeping,* sometimes occurs with wooden tubs. Keeping the water at its optimum level prevents staves from contracting. This keeps weeping to a minimum. If a leak occurs, you can easily repair it. See page 151.

WOODS USED FOR TUBS

Woods for hot tubs must be durable and resistant to decay and chemicals. Vertical-grain wood is preferred. This pattern maximizes the *swell factor* or *healing quality* of wood. All wood used for tubs must be kiln-dried or thoroughly seasoned.

The California Lumber Inspection Service of San Jose, California, tests various wood species for strength and decay resistance for the manufacturing of tubs. The service also classifies species by tree size.

The woods listed here all scored well in tests. The prices of each will vary according to availability in your area. Imported woods generally cost more than local ones. Redwood and red cedar are still the most popular woods for hot tubs.

Redwood—It's not surprising that redwood was the first wood used for hot tubs. It's been used in water tanks for at least a century. Redwood tubs are still the most common.

Commercial stands of redwood are found only in California. Its heartwood is decay-resistant and absorbs water well to form watertight joints. Redwood is also noted for its insulating qualities.

For about the first three months after a redwood tub is filled, natural *tannin* in the wood leaches out and discolors the water. Leaching also occurs with cedar, mahogany and some other wood species, but to a lesser degree. Leaching can be hastened, as described on page 148. Tannin is not considered harmful to soakers—see "Health Hazard from Redwood?" on page 22.

Redwood does not stay red forever. In a couple of seasons, it will weather to a silvery gray, which most people find attractive. Because wood is porous, chemicals can penetrate it, causing white deposits. These are harmless and can be removed by scrubbing.

Cedar—Several manufacturers make cedar hot tubs. The most common species used is *Western Red cedar.* It grows in the Pacific Northwest. This wood is resistant to decay. Some dealers claim it takes less time to leach tannin from cedar than from redwood. New and weathered, red cedar differs little from redwood in apperarance.

Some manufacturers emphasize the insulating value of cedar. Cedar has a higher *R-factor,* or *insulation rating,* than most other woods used for tubs. The higher the R-factor, the more effective the insulation. The R-factor of cedar is 1.29. Redwood is the standard at 1.0.

Also used for tubs, *Alaskan Yellow cedar* is a finely textured wood. It has a unique cellular structure that makes it durable, smooth and dense. It averages 100 growth rings per inch, compared to approximately 30 rings per inch in redwood. As standing timber, Alaskan Yellow cedar is distinctly yellow. But the milled lumber is almost white, similar to birch.

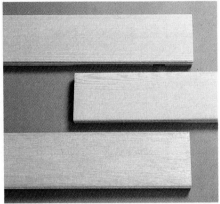

The most popular woods for hot tubs are redwood, top; red cedar, center; and mahogany, bottom.

Mahogany—Two types of mahogany are used in hot-tub manufacturing. Some manufacturers use imported *Philippine* or *Red Luan mahogany*. Mahogany is available in shades from bright red to white. *Honduras mahogany* is more expensive than Philippine or Luan mahogany. It's heavier and has a furniture-quality appearance.

The lumber can be bought in uniform thickness and length, but varies from 6 inches to 14 inches in width. The resulting waste factor makes mahogany quite expensive as a tub material. Mahogany leaches less than redwood.

Cypress—There are a number of cypress species. Those commonly used for lumber are native to swampy areas in the southeastern United States. Cypress is readily available as lumber in that region, less so in other parts of the country.

Cypress has appealing characteristics for manufacturers and buyers. It's durable and requires little maintenance. It is similar to redwood in decay resistance.

Cypress has excellent insulating properties, resulting in minimal heat loss. Leaching is not a problem because cypress has no tannic acid.

Finally, cypress is a beautiful wood. It ages to a light-gray patina, and has an attractive natural grain.

Alerce—This species of wood, pronounced *allure-see,* is from southern Chile. It's often referred to as *red cypress,* though it's not of the same family.

Alerce is flat-grained with a smooth, glasslike surface. It has a unique pattern of grain variations. It's dense with 98 growth rings per inch, but it is classified as a softwood.

Due to its density, alerce doesn't swell much when wet. Tubs made from this wood require more precise joinery.

Alerce has less tannin than redwood, but some water discoloration occurs initially.

Teak—Teak is a hardwood that is very dense. The boat-building industry has valued its strength and beauty for hundreds of years. Two species, *Burmese* and *Thai teak,* are generally classified together as *Indonesian teak.* Furniture- and cabinet-makers value teak for its beauty and intricate patterns.

The density of teak renders it almost impervious to water, rot or insects. It's been used in the manufacture of expensive tanning tanks that withstand highly caustic chemical solutions. The chemical balance of even a poorly maintained hot tub would not harm this wood. Teak hot tubs are expensive compared to other woods.

Jarrah—A member of the eucalyptus family, jarrah is a another dense wood. In its native land of Australia, jarrah is used for railroad ties. One manufacturer claims that jarrah has all the attributes of redwood without the discoloring tannic acid. It keeps its natural color when wet.

Bocote—This South American hardwood, pronounced *bow-caw-tee,* is even harder than teak, and about twice as expensive. For this reason, it's used only for custom orders. The wood is a beautiful light green with a

---

HEALTH HAZARD FROM REDWOOD?

Some hot-tub users worry that the tannic acid leaching from redwood tubs poses a health hazard. Their fears stem from the water color, which resembles root beer, during the leaching period.

The Spa and Tub division of the National Spa and Pool Institute commissioned a study on the potential toxicity of tannic acid in redwood tubs. The results of the study indicate that properly prepared and maintained redwood hot tubs *do not pose any health hazard to soakers.*

Dr. Vernon Singleton, a consultant at the University of California, Davis, noted in a report that tannin found in redwood is generally well tolerated by humans, even in food.

The durability of redwood, its relatively high tannin content and the high temperature of the water deter most microorganisms. Bacterial contamination is manageable through proper use of sanitizers.

brown tint, accentuated by black lines and bird's-eye whorls.

White Oak—This species is readily available in all parts of the United States. White oak is the only oak species recommended for hot tubs—and then only for indoor installations.

Pine—Hot tubs can also be made of *Northern Ontario pine,* also known as *golden pine.* Canadians use golden pine for whiskey barrels and distilling tanks. Golden pine is harder than most pine species and has a knotty appearance.

CHOOSING A GOOD-QUALITY TUB

When shopping for wooden tubs, look for good quality in materials and workmanship. Pay special attention to the quality of the wood itself.

The following is a list of characteristics to look for when shopping for a hot tub. You may not find all these features in any one tub.

Wood—Look for tight, vertical-grain lumber without defects, such as knots, decay, splits or milling imperfections. Sides, bottom and seats should be of the same quality wood. No matter which wood species you choose, always look for tubs made from the *heartwood* of that species. Heartwood is the darker-colored wood cut from the center of the tree. It resists decay better than the lighter-colored sapwood, and will generally last longer.

Staves—Joints should be tight with no interior crevices where bacteria and algae can grow. Drainage joints between the staves on the tub's exterior are acceptable. The stave's interior curvature can provide furniture-finish smoothness if desired. Individual staves should be formed from straight, vertical-grain lumber. Staves should be at least 1-5/8 inches thick. Tubs with thick staves will last longer and retain heat better.

Croze—Grooves in the staves that hold the floorboards, called the *croze,* should be milled so staves come in full contact with the floorboards. The area below the croze should be thick and wide enough to prevent splitting. Edges around the croze should be routed or precision cut to reduce splintering.

Floorboards—The ends of the floorboards should be routed to prevent splitting. Floorboards should be sanded smooth to reduce splintering.

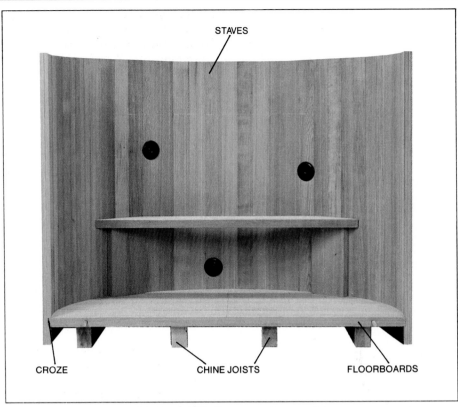

Cutaway of hot tub shows joinery details. Tongue-and-groove joints on staves help prevent leaks and make assembly easier. Floorboards are doweled together for added strength.

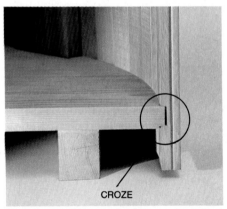

Staves should come in full, even contact with the floorboards at the croze joint. Here, a small gap has been left between the ends of the floorboards and the staves for wood expansion when the tub is filled with water.

Bands Or Hoops—Good-quality tubs have rustproof, well-finished bands or hoops. Any band or hoop protrusions should be capped for both appearance and safety.

Benches—These shouldn't interfere with cleaning the tub floor or with water circulation. There's a wide variety of seat types: multilevel for children and adults, full or partial surround seating, and step access for children.

Hoop ends protruding from the hoop lugs should be capped, as shown here.

Screws—High-quality stainless-steel or brass screws are best.

Dowels—Predrilled dowel construction looks natural. Dowel ends can be hidden or exposed.

Fittings—Ask about torque measurements for adjusting wall fittings so swollen wood will not break the jet fittings.

Dimensions—Determine the specific dimensions of your tub. Find out where the tub diameter measurement has been taken—at water surface level, the tub rim, midway on the staves or any other location. Is it an inside or outside diameter measurement? Does it include the thickness of the hoops? Is the height the total stave height or is it measured from the croze? What's the interior height? These questions are important because one manufacturer's "4x6" tub may be larger or smaller than another's.

Skimmers—These skim leaves and other debris from the water surface. Skimmers made specifically for hot tubs are available.

Vacuuming Equipment—Used to clean debris from bottom and sides of spa or tub. Some types attach to skimmer, others operate using an ordinary garden hose.

BEFORE YOU BUY

Now that you know what to look for in a quality spa or tub, it's time to consider where you'll buy it. Like any new industry, the spa and hot-tub business has had its share of disreputable operators. If you want to avoid problems, do some advance research. This simple point can't be stressed too strongly.

For the amount of money you'll spend, you can hardly consider a spa or hot tub an impulse item. Your best insurance is to buy the highest quality spa or hot tub you can afford, from the most qualified and reputable dealer you can find. Start your shopping in the Yellow Pages of your phone book. Find out which dealers in your area have the best selection of spas and tubs.

You'll probably buy your spa's or tub's support equipment, such as heater, pump, filter, and equipment from the same dealer. Before you shop, become familiar with what's available. Information on buying support equipment starts on page 75.

COMPARING MANUFACTURERS

When shopping for a spa or tub, find out how long the manufacturer, as well as the dealer, has been in business—the longer the better. Make a few calls to people who repair pool and spa equipment. They'll be able to tell you which models need the fewest repairs. The manufacturer's warranty is often a good indication of quality. Find out what parts are covered and under what conditions. Also note how long the warranty lasts. Beware of unrealistically long warranties. If the manufacturer goes out of business, the warranty will be useless.

CHOOSING YOUR DEALER

When you shop for a spa or hot tub, shop for the best dealer. A reputable dealer will take time to give you as much information as possible and answer all your questions candidly. Dealers know that the best advertisement is a satisfied customer.

The dealer you choose should supply references of at least three satisfied customers. Check them all. Call the Better Business Bureau to see if any customers have filed complaints against the dealer. Also ask the dealer for credit references—especially if the company is to do the installation. An established, financially solvent company is more likely to honor contracts and guarantees.

A good dealer tells potential customers what to expect in terms of maintenance and problems.

Check to see if the dealer belongs to any trade associations or local contractor's associations. This is often an indication of the dealer's stability in the community. Find out if the dealer is a member of the National Spa and Pool Institute (NSPI). This is the national trade organization of the spa and swimming pool industry. NSPI members are expected to conform to the organization's quality standards for business ethics and construction practices. For more information on the NSPI, see page 154.

When the contract is signed, the dealer should make it clear what you can expect from him. He should be very explicit on what his responsibilities are as far as maintenance and what is covered in the warranty.

The contract should include a clause on maintenance so that there is no question as to who's responsible in the event of equipment failure. A good dealer will caution you about the cost of repairing or replacing equipment if you don't maintain it properly.

Some dealers have designed sales programs to inform their customers of all the steps involved in buying and installing a spa or tub. A few even offer complete installation instructions for do-it-yourselfers and will gladly answer questions during installation.

The final and perhaps most important question to ask a prospective dealer is how payments are handled. Some dealers will arrange progress payments. If the dealer is also installing the unit, payments may be made as each phase of the work is completed.

A dealer doesn't necessarily have to meet all of the mentioned requirements to be considered fair and reputable. However, by checking references and asking questions, you'll get a good impression of which dealers are reputable and which aren't. When you have a list of potential dealers, you can start seriously shopping for the best deal.

WHO INSTALLS IT?

Installing a spa or wooden hot tub requires a working knowledge of masonry, plumbing, carpentry and electrical wiring. Whether or not you can do part or all of the installation yourself depends on your knowledge of these skills and the amount of technical information available from your dealer. Your other options are to hire a qualified, licensed contractor specializing in spa or tub installation, or let the dealer handle the work.

DOING IT YOURSELF

This book offers only general guidelines for installing prefabricated spas and hot tubs. You'll also need additional installation guidelines for the unit you've chosen. These should be available from your dealer.

Even with the best instructions, correctly installing a spa or hot tub demands careful work. Before you decide to do any or all of the installation, read through the chapter "Installing a Spa or Hot Tub," pages 103-105, to see what's involved.

If you're a casual do-it-yourselfer, you can hire a qualified, licensed contractor.

For those who want to save money, some dealers recommend a combination program. The owner does the less-complicated tasks, such as excavation, pouring foundation slabs,

Most hot-tub manufacturers offer kits with easy-to-follow instructions. Tools for assembly are available at hardware stores.

preliminary plumbing and building decking and surrounding structures. The contractor does the main plumbing, gas and electrical hookups.

If you decide to do some of the work yourself, make sure this is written into the contract. It should clearly specify both your responsibilities and those of the installer. For more on contracts, see page 27.

Another option for spa buyers is to buy a preplumbed unit. Some manufacturers plumb their spas at the factory. In other cases, the dealer may plumb the spa after it's delivered to the showroom. Either way, buying your spa preplumbed makes installation considerably easier. If you buy a preplumbed spa, ask the dealer to fill it with water to make sure there are no leaks in the plumbing system. Preplumbed spas require extra care in transport so plumbing is not damaged. *Never lift or carry the unit by its plumbing fixtures.*

If you do the entire installation yourself, you'll be responsible for getting the building permit and arranging for building inspections. Don't overlook these two phases. The building permit and inspections ensure that

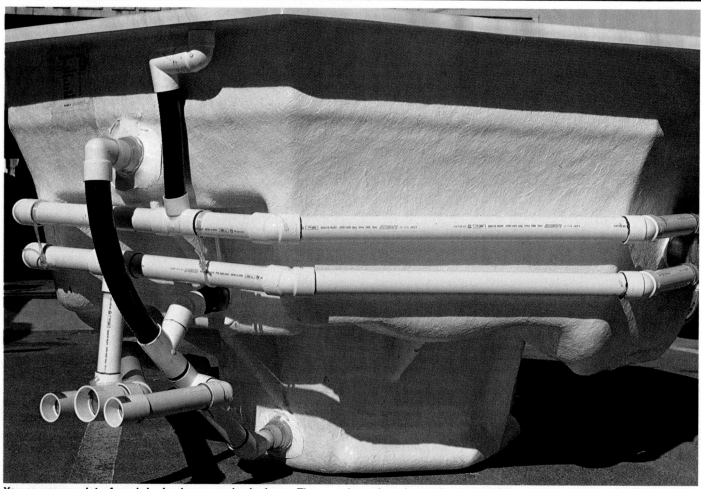

You can save a lot of work by buying a preplumbed spa. The one shown here is preplumbed for jets, skimmer, drain and safety suction fitting. Note how pipe ends are aligned and color-coded for easy hookup to support-equipment lines.

the installation meets local codes, and above all, is safe. Without them, you may have legal or other problems later. For more information on permits and inspections, see page 105.

Caution—Spas and hot tubs bring people, water and electricity close together—a potentially dangerous situation if you don't wire and plumb the unit correctly. For this reason, it's safer to have a licensed contractor or subcontractor wire and plumb the unit, even if you do the rest of the installation yourself.

HIRING A CONTRACTOR

If you decide to have your unit installed professionally, it will pay to do a little research before choosing a contractor. Some spa and hot-tub dealers offer installation as part of their services. Others will recommend contractors they have worked with. You may choose to buy the spa or tub from a dealer and then shop around for your own contractor.

The first step for anyone thinking of hiring a contractor is to check with the Contractor's State License Board. Verify the contractor's license and see if the company is bonded and has insurance for workman's compensation. This simple procedure can save you many headaches. For information regarding a contractor's performance and reliability, contact the Better Business Bureau.

Next, ask for references from other customers in the area. It not only allows you to see the quality of the contractor's work, but also to talk with the spa or hot-tub owner about whether or not the work was done according to schedule.

OTHER PROFESSIONAL HELP

You may want to hire a landscape architect or designer, concrete mason or carpenter to complete your installation.

A spa or hot tub is a permanent part of your landscape—one that should add to the value of your home. It's a good idea to do everything you can to make sure you get the most out of the addition. A qualified landscape architect can draw an initial plan for locating your spa or tub. He can also plan decks, patios and lighting, and choose appropriate plants.

Most landscape architects and designers charge by the hour for initial design work. The owner can then work from the design himself or hire a landscape crew to do the work for a set fee. On major landscape projects, you may want the landscape architect or designer to oversee the work.

You may be interested only in plants. Some large nurseries will work with your plan for a small fee—sometimes even for free—if you agree to buy all your plants from them. Their advice is often invaluable. It helps you avoid possible expensive mistakes that may have to be corrected years later.

Concrete masons and carpenters can install concrete patios or wooden decks surrounding the spa or tub. They work on an hourly basis or for a set fee.

Wood or masonry decking, as mentioned on pages 36-44, is a project within the abilities of most do-it-yourselfers. If you want to save money, this is where you can probably do it easiest.

GETTING BIDS

Always get bids from several competing firms. You'll find it educational as well as economical.

The lowest bid isn't always the best deal. But low bids don't always reflect shoddy or incomplete work, either. When getting bids, always ask for a detailed estimate of materials and services provided. The estimate should include a cost breakdown, itemizing materials and labor for each phase of the job.

Material and labor costs are constantly changing. For this reason, many contractors will only guarantee their bids for a specified time. Find out how long the contractor will honor the price quoted.

WRITING A CONTRACT

Some aspects of contracts with pool or spa dealers, installers and contractors may differ, but certain basics

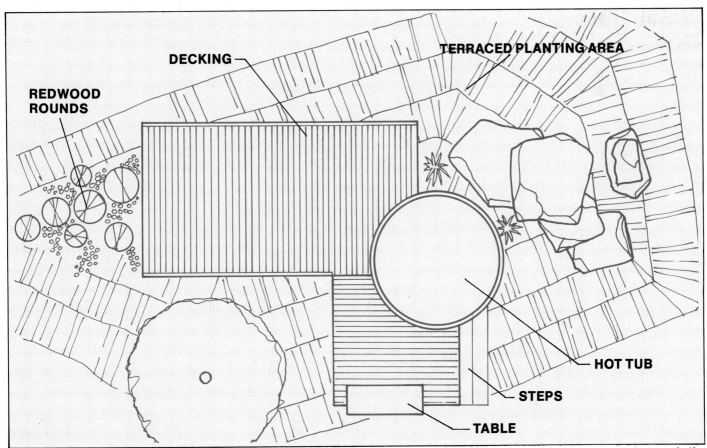

A professionally designed landscape around your spa or tub may require a larger initial investment, but it can save time and money in the long run.

Architect's plans are helpful in creating an attractive spa or tub environment. Once you have a set of plans, you can work from them yourself or have the architect subcontract the work.

always apply. Any written contract should include the following:
● An approximate date to start installation or construction.
● A completion date.
● What happens if the project is not completed on time.
● Specifications for all parts and equipment—actual model numbers, sizes, manufacturer's name and so on.
● Guarantees and warranties for specified equipment.
● A schedule of payments, with the last payment tied to the *completion* of the project, or better, slightly after.
● A description of any aftercare. Some spa and hot-tub dealers and contractors offer checkups after the installation is completed to make sure everything is running correctly. Others do not. Find out about this before you sign the contract. In addition, you may want to specify allowable working hours and access routes.

Check to make sure your contract complies with local laws!

AVOIDING PROBLEMS AFTER INSTALLATION

The best assurance of having a spa or tub properly installed is having the best-possible contractor do the work. If you decide on a professional installation, you must trust the person you hire. But it never hurts to keep a close eye on the project as it progresses.

When overseeing the installation, it will help if you know the steps involved. Starting on page 103 are step-by-step procedures for installing a spa or hot tub. Become familiar with these procedures. You'll be better able to spot something before it becomes a problem.

Don't hesitate to ask installers to explain things you don't understand. If something bothers you, question it. After all, you're the one who must live with the completed project.

Before your spa or tub is installed, let your insurance agent know about the pending addition. You may want to make adjustments in your policy to be certain you're covered.

FINANCING A SPA OR TUB

There's more than one way to spread out financing payments. There may be several options available that you're not aware of.

HOME-IMPROVEMENT LOANS

This is the most common method for financing spas and hot tubs. Home-improvement loans are available from banks, savings and loan companies and sometimes credit unions.

In some cases, home-improvement loans may be *unsecured*. This means it does *not* require collateral such as real estate or other securities.

The term of the loan is usually fairly short, from five to seven years, and the amount moderate, around $5,000. Larger loans with longer payback periods are available if you decide to secure the loan.

When shopping for a loan, start at the bank where you already do business. Some banks offer better rates to customers with existing accounts.

If you belong to a credit union, don't forget to give them a call.

HOME-EQUITY LOANS

You can capitalize on the amount your house has increased in value since you purchased it. The amount of *equity* you have in a house is determined by subtracting the amount you owe on your house from its current appraised value.

You can refinance your house—take out a larger mortgage and pay off the old balance. This leaves you with excess cash to use as you see fit. But this method has drawbacks. You'll be saddled with higher house payments and higher interest rates on the new loan.

Another type of equity loan, known as a *second mortgage,* is a high-interest, short-term loan. In most cases, borrowers can get a loan for as much as 75% or 80% of the equity they have in their house.

SIGNATURE LOANS

Many banks offer a variety of simplified loan procedures. Among them is the *signature loan*. With this loan, the preapproved applicant can borrow up to $5,000 on his or her signature alone. If you have a good relationship with your bank, and a good credit rating, you can probably qualify for a signature loan. Preferred customers may get loans at somewhat less than the going rate.

PASSBOOK LOANS

You may be able to use your savings account as collateral for a loan. In most cases, customers can borrow up to 90% of the amount in the savings account, at rates 2% to 3% above the current interest rate on the account. Because the savings account continues to accrue interest, net cost to the borrower is reasonable.

COLLATERAL LOANS

Sometimes, you can use securities, cars or real estate as collateral for a loan. It's not uncommon for these loans to carry a lower interest rate than signature loans.

INCOME-TAX LOANS

Some banks and finance companies will give you a short-term loan, based on your expected income-tax refund.

LIFE-INSURANCE LOANS

Most insurance policies with a cash value allow the holder to borrow up to 95% of the accrued value—often at reasonable rates. Although the interest must be paid back each year, you can pay back the principal whenever you choose.

3

Creating a Special Environment

Raised planter bed is incorporated into the design of this spa and brick patio. Spa-side plantings help break up harsh, symmetrical lines of brickwork.

Spas and hot tubs are wonderful by themselves. They're even more enjoyable when you create a *special environment* around them.

There are two basic goals in landscaping around a spa or hot tub. One is to take care of practical considerations. These include privacy, protection from the weather, easy and safe access, lights for night use and protection for children. The other is to make the surroundings attractive and inviting. This is done by the careful selection and placement of plants and surrounding structures, and by locating the spa or tub with existing surroundings in mind.

WHERE TO PUT YOUR SPA OR TUB

Where should you install your spa or tub? The answer involves a

Left: This complete structural environment includes multilevel decking, railing, seating, planter boxes and overhead shade screen.

Privacy is an important consideration in selecting a location for your spa or tub. With the help of screens and plantings you can make your spa or tub a secluded retreat.

An unused side yard can be an excellent location. Spas and hot tubs fit into surprisingly small yard spaces.

number of decisions. When you've made them, you can then pick several prospective sites.

Do you want the spa or tub indoors or out? Though most are put under open sky, this may limit their use in climates with severe winters. For year-round use in these climates, the spa or tub should be fully protected.

OUTDOORS

Soaking in a spa or tub can be an in-

timate experience. Most people want a certain amount of privacy. How comfortable they feel when soaking outdoors depends on the spa's or tub's location in the yard and the landscaping around it.

Check which spots in your yard are out of the neighbors' view. If these areas are unacceptable for other reasons, plan to add screening when you do choose a spot.

Don't rule out front or side yards. With proper landscaping, these areas can be just as intimate and attractive as a backyard location.

The time of day you'll be using the unit will help determine the site. If maximum use will be at night, exposure to the sun is not critical. If maximum use will be during daylight hours, you must plan more carefully.

A southern exposure will receive the most sun; a northern exposure the least. A spa or tub with an eastern exposure will catch the early morning sun. A western exposure may allow you to watch the sunset.

Wind is not only uncomfortable for soakers, but also blows leaves and other debris into the spa or tub. Cool winds blowing across the water's surface will rob heat from the spa or tub. This means the heater must work overtime to keep water at the desired temperature.

Look for sites sheltered from strong, prevailing winds. These may be areas protected by mature shrubs or trees, or nearby structures, such as buildings or fences. To help find these sites, attach strips of cloth or ribbon to 3-foot stakes. Place them around the yard on a windy day. They'll indicate wind direction and force at various sites.

How far from the house should you place your unit? A closer location may ensure more use. This is especially true if you plan to use it primarily for a quick soak before retiring. If children are going to use the spa or tub, it's a good idea to place it in full view of the house.

If you live on a sloping or contoured lot, avoid locating in-ground spas or tubs in natural drainage areas or runoff slopes. You'll want irrigation and rain water to drain *away* from the unit, not *into* it.

Every yard offers several potential sites. Walk around the area. Think how it would feel to be in a spa or tub in different locations. If your spa is going to be sunk into the ground, get down on your hands and knees. See what the location looks like from that vantage point.

Stray off the beaten path to see what the view is like from seldom-used areas. Compare potential views beyond your property. It's a real bonus to have a panoramic view when you're sitting in a spa or tub.

Is there a particular spot in your yard where you already feel comfortable? This could be under a spreading tree, or on a deck off your bedroom. A site that offers some enclosure and security can be ideal for your spa or tub. But keep in mind that a site under or around shrubs or trees will increase cleanup from falling leaves.

Aesthetics aside, remember that the farther your spa or tub is from the source of water and electricity or gas, the more it will cost to run lines to it.

Finally, check local codes and ordinances before making your final decision. They may require a spa or tub to be placed a certain distance from property lines, fences or neighboring houses. These setback distances may also govern the height of a fence or screen surrounding the unit. Your local building department can supply this information.

This spa room was designed for easy access to the pool outside.

INDOORS

The popularity of hot tubs and spas has spread from the West Coast to the colder climates. Many Midwesterners and Easterners are deciding to install spas and tubs indoors. Many combine them with a sauna or exercise equipment to create a complete home-fitness center.

If you want the spa or tub in your house, you can convert existing floor space to accept the unit, or add a spa or hot tub room to the house. Both op-

If you're fortunate enough to have a good view from your yard, locate the spa or tub to take best advantage of it!

Almost any room in the house can be remodeled into a spa room. Color of fiberglass spa blends well with ornate woodwork in this Victorian parlor. Large mirror creates illusion of space in small area.

Textured-concrete spa room is a perfect environment for moisture-loving plants. Adjoining dressing room leads to house.

tions generally involve remodeling, unless you choose a portable spa as described on pages 18-19.

If you want an indoor spa or tub in the yard, simply put a room around it. You can use conventional building methods, or buy a prefabricated greenhouse or dome-type enclosure. For more information on enclosures, see pages 49-51.

Many homeowners who add spa or tub rooms to the house favor the greenhouse-type enclosure. These can be custom-designed or bought in prefabricated kit form. Construction costs are usually less than more conventional additions. Plants thrive in the bright, humid atmosphere, making a beautiful environment.

Many of the considerations for locating outdoor units apply to indoor units as well. If the spa or tub room is an addition to the house, consider the effect its location will have on traffic through the house. How will the spa or tub room affect your family's household routine? Will access routes disrupt activities in other rooms? Will the room be easily accessible to all who'll use the spa or tub? Is the room convenient to dressing areas?

These considerations also apply to the addition of a spa or tub to an existing room. Consider the remodeling necessary to make the room acceptable. Floors in most homes are de-

signed to support about 40 pounds per square foot. A spa or tub filled with water and people can exert 200 to 300 pounds per square foot—much more than most floors can handle. Check with the local building department to find out what type of reinforcement is needed to support the added weight.

With all indoor spas and tubs, plan to vent the increased humidity to the outdoors.

To prevent humidity buildup, you'll need an exhaust fan that can change the total air volume of the room in 6 minutes. Floors should be non-slippery when wet and all surfaces should be moisture-resistant.

Finally, plan for locking doors leading to the spa or tub room to keep youngsters from unsupervised use.

PUT YOUR PLAN ON PAPER

When you have several sites in mind, make a scale drawing of the installation and surrounding area. This will help you consider the possibilities of each location. You can refer to the drawing when designing the landscape around the spa or tub.

To make a scale drawing, you'll need graph paper, pencils, a straight-edge, and a 50- or 100-foot tape measure. A large sheet of 1/4-inch graph paper is best for most plans. A convenient scale is 1/4 inch equals 1 foot.

An existing plot or site plan of your property will help you with your drawing. These plans usually show lot dimensions and orientation to north, location of underground utilities and sometimes the relationship of the house to the lot. If you don't have a plot plan, check with the designer or builder of your house. If your property was professionally landscaped, the designer may have plans that show exact locations of existing plantings and garden structures.

Begin measuring the dimensions of your yard from a particular line. This is called the *base line*. A base line can be a lot line, one side of your house, a fence or the edge of a walkway.

When you draw the base line, locate it so the whole drawing will fit on one sheet of paper. If you use one side of your house as the base line, measure from each corner to the end of the lot or yard and to the lot lines on both sides. Transfer these measurements to the paper and connect the points to form the yard boundaries.

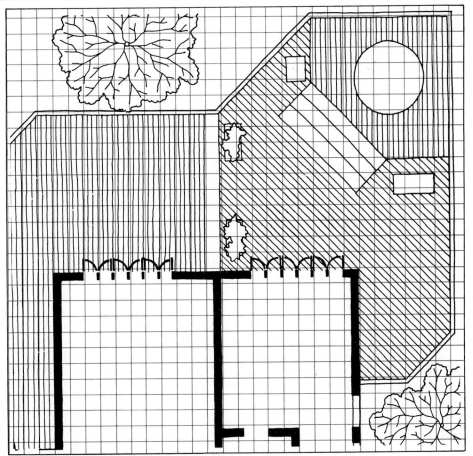

A scale drawing will help you visualize exact locations of the various elements of your spa or hot-tub installation. You can also use the drawing to help estimate materials.

If the spa or tub is not convenient to the house, include a dressing area in your plans. This outdoor dressing room includes a shower for cooling off after a hot soak.

After you've drawn outside dimensions, add all other important features in your yard. Always measure them from the same base line. Include trees, patios, walkways, water spigots, electrical outlets, garden beds and borders. Draw in anything else that may influence location and design. This may include path of sun, direction of prevailing winds, and location of underground pipes and wires.

When you have this information on paper, it becomes your base map. Redraw it more neatly, if necessary. If the lot slopes, make a tracing-paper overlay showing contours and natural drainage areas in the yard.

Tape a piece of tracing paper over the top of the finished base plan. Sketch possible locations for your spa or hot tub. Consider the pros and cons of each choice.

At this point, it's easy and cost-free to change your mind as often as you like. Take a little extra time in the planning stage. You should end up with a location that's best for you, your family and neighbors.

THE STRUCTURAL ENVIRONMENT

The structures surrounding a spa or tub can be as simple as a few concrete steppingstones or wood boards leading to the unit. More sophisticated surroundings may include a wood deck or masonry patio, fences and screens, plant supports, benches, lighting or all of these. Or, the unit may be partially sheltered by a gazebo or completely enclosed in a room. These and other manmade elements make up a spa or tub's *structural environment.*

When planning the structural environment, think about coordinating all the elements. For example, a wood deck, benches, planters and vertical and overhead shade screens can be integrated into one structure. Choose materials carefully to create harmonious surroundings. Try to visualize how colors and textures of different materials go together, and how they relate to your house and other surroundings.

Brick makes an excellent decking material around spas and hot tubs. Porous common brick used here provides a non-slip walking surface.

WHAT GOES UNDERFOOT

Put a walking surface around your spa or tub that will withstand outdoor conditions—especially water. The surface should be non-slippery and easy to wash off. It should harmonize with existing garden or patio structures and pavements. It should be comfortable to walk and lie on.

Suitable surfaces include *brick, wood, concrete, paving stones, tile* and a masonry product called *Kool Decking*.

The two most popular choices are brick and wood. They appear *natural* in a garden setting. They're attractive and lasting, but are comparatively expensive surfaces.

Brick—A brick patio is a good project for a beginning do-it-yourselfer. Work can be done in different stages.

Bricks come in many textures and colors. The two most popular for patios are smooth-surfaced *face bricks* and the more porous *common bricks*. *Used bricks* make an attractive surface, but these must be chosen carefully because the rough surfaces of some may be hard on bare feet. In all cases, choose a brick surface that's easy on feet, yet not slippery when wet.

Perhaps the biggest drawback is weight. A load of bricks for even a small project is heavy. Transporting them can be difficult.

It's best to have bricks delivered to your house and stacked as near to the project as possible. When estimating quantity, plan to use five bricks per square foot. That number allows extras to compensate for breakage.

Brick and tile make a striking combination in this multilevel spa. Cap tiles around spa edges were custom-made to match brick color.

The most common method of installation is to place bricks on a level bed of sand. For more solid or permanent patios, bricks are laid on a bed of concrete mortar. The sand method is more than adequate for most purposes.

A brick patio should slope slightly away from the spa or tub to allow surface drainage. When planting around a brick patio, select plants whose root systems won't disrupt the bricks.

Wood—Redwood and cedar are the two best wood choices for outdoor decks. They're attractive and naturally resistant to decay. Fir, pine, spruce and other softwoods can be used if they've been treated with a clear wood preservative. Most lumberyards carry lumber that's been pressure-treated with preservative. Most pressure-treated woods will outlast redwood and cedar. If pressure-treated woods aren't available in your area, treat ordinary lumber with a clear-wood preservative. Soaking the wood overnight gives more protection than surface brushing, spraying or dipping. Most preservatives are toxic, so use them with care.

It's not always necessary to build an elaborate, permanent structure. Sometimes all you need are a few portable decks that keep feet clean and dry. For any deck, leave a little space between the surface boards. This allows water to drain. For tips on deck building, see pages 40-45.

Concrete—This material is a mixture of cement, sand and gravel. Concrete patios can be made in many shapes, sizes and surface textures. Whether

Clean, uncluttered look of this concrete patio makes the spa a focal point in the yard.

Multilevel redwood deck surrounds this older hot tub and wine-vat cool pool in foreground. In several years, the deck will weather to match wood color of tub.

Large expanses of masonry work can be made more interesting by using contrasting colors. Here, red bricks accent spa, pool and slump-block wall. Decking is exposed aggregate.

Exposed aggregate is more natural-looking than finished concrete. It also reflects less sunlight, making it easier on the eyes.

you want a smooth or rough surface texture depends on how you finish it. On *exposed-aggregate* finishes, gravel in the concrete is left exposed on the surface. Exposed aggregate is more natural-looking than smooth-finish concrete. It also provides a low-glare surface.

Small concrete patios and walkways can be owner-built. For small projects, dry-mixed concrete comes in 90-pound sacks—you add the water. For larger surfaces, have ready-mixed concrete delivered and poured in place. Make sure the site is accessible to a large truck. You can do the finish work yourself, or hire a masonry contractor. Companies that carry ready-mixed concrete are listed in the Yellow Pages under "Concrete, Ready Mixed."

Concrete patios require wood forms to hold the concrete in place until it

Flagstone makes an attractive, if somewhat rough, walking surface.

Creek stones leading into the water give soakers the sensation of walking into a natural stream or river. The less adventurous can enter this spa from the quarry-tile patio in the background.

Tile patio gives this spa installation a formal look. Patio tiles have a slip-proof surface.

sets. Forms for curving patios are made from thin, flexible boards. Have all forms built prior to ordering or buying concrete.

Paving Stones—Surface possibilities with stone are limitless. Paving stones range from small pebbles to large flagstones. They can be set in concrete, mortar, sand or soil. Planning requirements for paving stones around spas and tubs are the same as for other materials.

Tile—Elegant but expensive, tile is often used in conjunction with other surfaces around spas and tubs. Two types are used for patios—quarry tile and patio tile. Patio tile is less expensive, but more irregular in shape. Many kinds of patio tile can be used indoors or out.

This hillside deck seems to float among the treetops. On steep lots like this one, deck design should be left to a professional.

Multilevel deck provides separate activity areas, seating and easy access to hot tub.

Use unglazed tiles with a non-slip surface—other kinds are too slick to use around spas and tubs. Tiles can be laid over concrete or level, compacted sand. On concrete, tiles can have mortared joints. They give the surface a more finished appearance. If mortared, joints should be 1/4- to 1/2-inch wide.

INSTALLING A DECK

The two most important things in building a deck are *sound design* and *good workmanship*. Most decks around spas and tubs require only basic carpentry skills and woodworking knowledge. Decks requiring more extensive building knowledge include hillside decks, second-story decks or any deck over 4 feet tall that must support the full weight of the spa or tub. These are best left to experts.

Design Points—Many people envision a flat, simple deck around a spa or hot tub. But for a few dollars more, you can have a three-dimensional deck that will enhance the beauty and value of your home. Multilevel decks are especially adaptable to above-ground spa and tub installations. They can provide built-in seating or separate, intimate areas for sunning before or after a soak. The top level can be flush with the rim of the spa or tub for easy access. If tall enough, these decks can also shelter support equipment or provide storage areas for accessories.

Proper scale is important to providing a balanced-looking installation. The size and shape of the deck should complement the spa or tub and fit into the surrounding landscape. This is especially important if your lot is irregular in shape or the site has existing landscape elements you wish to keep.

Make a scale drawing of the deck before you lay it out in the yard. See "Put Your Plan on Paper," page 34. The deck will look good in the yard if you can make it look good on paper.

You can save money by designing your deck to take best advantage of

Octagonal deck was designed to complement lines of in-ground fiberglass spa. Wood is pressure-treated with preservative to resist decay.

standard lumber dimensions. Oddly proportioned decks not only create design problems, but they waste lumber. If a deck requires specially milled lumber, the effect created may not justify the added cost.

A key element in the design of a multilevel deck is the use of *headers* or *fascia boards* around the perimeter. The drawing on page 43 shows the location of these and other deck components. These boards help hide the deck's substructure—joists, beams and posts—and protect ends of joist and decking boards from the weather. They also give the deck a finished look. The width of these boards depends on the height of the deck level and how much of the substructure can be seen from eye level. Normally, the board's bottom edge extends 2 inches below the bottom edges of the joists, as shown in the drawing on page 43.

If deck is 4 feet high or more, you may want to hide the substructure with a vertical screen. A latticework screen will do this, yet allow sufficient ventilation under the deck to keep the substructure from decaying. Plantings also make good screens.

Structural Points—There are two approaches to use in building a deck for a spa or tub. The easiest is to build the deck *around* the spa or tub, after the unit is installed. If this approach is used for a hot tub, make sure you leave enough space between the decking and tub to allow for swelling when the tub is filled with water. A 1-inch gap between deck boards and tub sides should be adequate.

The second approach, which is used more often for tubs than for spas, is to build the deck first, then place the tub on top of it. This approach requires a much stronger deck to support the additional weight. The higher the deck surface is above the ground, the more complex its supporting structure becomes. Even low-level decks must have a strong foundation and substructure if they're to support the weight of the water-filled tub. Footings, posts, beams and joists must be larger and spaced close together, as described below.

It's usually more practical to use a separate foundation for the spa or tub. But if your plans call for a deck to support the unit, first find out the weight of the spa or tub filled with water and people. Then calculate how much weight per square foot will be exerted on the deck surface under the spa or tub. To figure pounds exerted per square foot, divide the overall weight of the unit by its bottom surface area in square feet.

Example: A 300-gallon tub filled with water and people weighs 7,500 pounds. The bottom surface area is 25 square feet. 7,500 ÷ 25 = 300. You need a deck that can support 300 pounds per square foot.

Once you know span and spacing re-quirements for the load the deck must carry, check local building codes to determine the type of substructure needed to support the unit.

Anatomy Of A Deck—Foundation, substructure and decking surface are the three basic parts of a deck. The *foundation* consists of poured-concrete *footings* and precast concrete *piers* or metal *post anchors*. See drawing on page 44. Elements of the *substructure* include *posts, beams* and *joists*. Depending on design, the substructure may also require *bracing*. The *decking surface* is generally 2-inch-thick lumber in any standard width. The drawing on the facing page shows how all these elements fit together in a simple deck.

The concrete foundation must support the entire weight of the deck. Footing size is determined by deck weight, type and slope of soil, and weight the deck must hold. Your local building department can tell you the required footing size.

Low railing around redwood deck helps define spa area within the yard. Small size of deck allows room for planting beds and lawn.

Generally, a 1-foot-square by 1-foot-deep footing is adequate. In cold climates, footings must extend below the frost line. Deeper footings may also be needed for hillside decks, as shown in the drawing below. It's best to have a soil engineer test soil stability on a steep incline or a site near a cliff. This will tell you if there's a need for extensive engineering and foundation work.

Concrete piers keep wood posts elevated slightly above ground level to prevent them from decaying. If piers aren't used, metal post anchors are set directly in the footings See drawing on page 44. If you use post anchors, make sure the footings extend several inches above ground level.

One of the most-common mistakes made in deck construction is incorrect sizing and placement of substructure members. Beam size depends on how far apart posts are spaced. Larger beams can span greater distances—

Deck Components

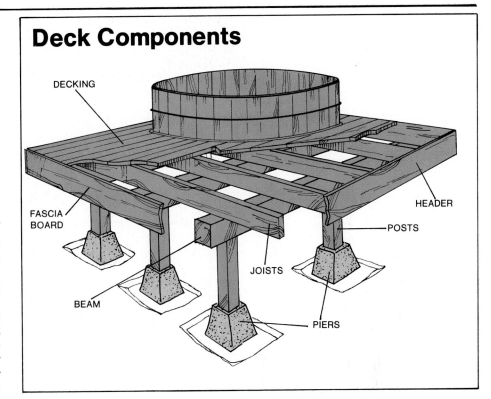

DECKING

FASCIA BOARD

BEAM

HEADER

POSTS

JOISTS

PIERS

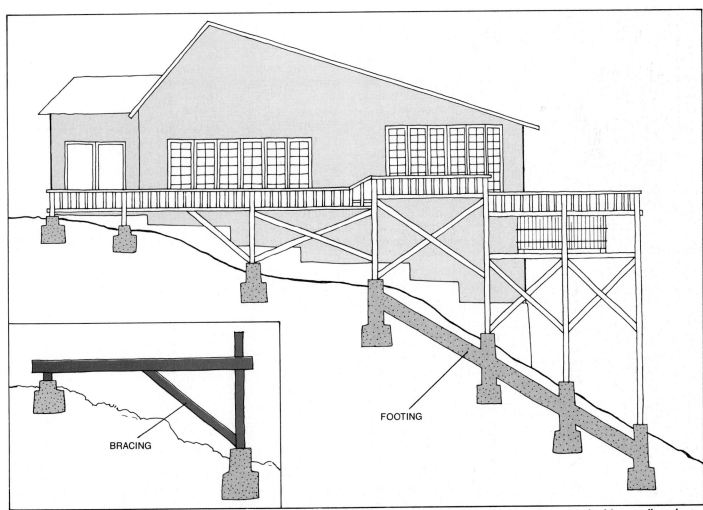

BRACING

FOOTING

Hillside decks on steep lots often require extensive foundations, as shown here. Ground stability should be checked by a soil engineer. Deck will require additional bracing to hold weight of spa or hot tub.

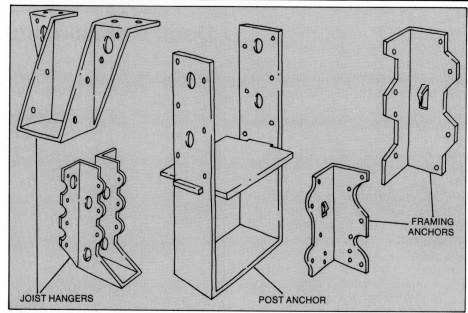

Metal fasteners are used to join various deck members. They make a stronger joint than simply nailing pieces together.

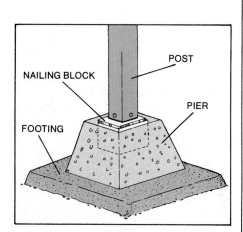

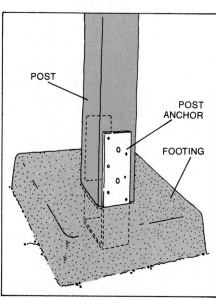

Piers or post anchors set in concrete footings support the entire weight of the deck. Proper spacing is crucial.

they require fewer posts to support them. The same holds true for joists and decking boards. Both are sized according to the span they must cross. As mentioned earlier, sizes and spans depend on the weight the deck must carry. Span charts are available at most lumberyards and local building departments. Use one when figuring sizing and spacing.

Another common mistake in deck building is failure to allow for proper ventilation underneath the deck. If the deck is close to the ground, stagnant air plus water from the spa or tub can cause dry rot. Any wood members in contact with the ground are susceptible to termite infestation. To help prevent these problems, use redwood or pressure-treated fir for all substructure members. Leave as much air space as possible around the deck's perimeter.

Many in-ground spas require very low decking. In such cases, joists, also called *stringers*, rest directly on the foundation piers. The decking is then nailed to the joists. No posts or beams are used. To avoid dry rot, allow at least 4 inches of space between the joists and the ground.

Building A Simple Deck—If you plan to build a simple deck around your spa or tub, the following tips will be helpful.

When selecting wood for the deck surface, look at the good side of the board. This way, you can choose good pieces from lower grades of lumber

and save money. Check for unsightly gouges and splinters that are potentially dangerous to bare feet. Check the ends for splits too large to be cut off economically.

Nails and other metal hardware for decks should be rust-resistant. Stainless-steel and aluminum nails are best for the decking surface. Wood acidity causes steel and galvanized nails to rust, staining the wood. Good-quality galvanized nails or vinyl-coated common nails, called *sinkers,* are adequate for building the substructure.

The preferred way to join substructure members is to use metal fasteners. Fasteners include various types of joist hangers, post caps, saddle fittings and straps. The most commonly used fasteners are shown above. They're available at lumberyards and home-improvement centers.

The step-by-step sequence on the next page shows the basic procedures for installing a simple deck around a spa or tub.

**FENCES AND
GARDEN SCREENS**

Security, privacy, shade and wind control are some of the things fences and garden screens offer bathers. In effect, they can take the place of shrubs or trees. Fences and screens can be permanent or temporary, stationary or mobile. Temporary fences or screens can offer protection until screen plants are established.

Building a Low-level Deck

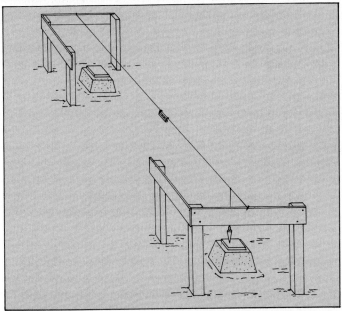

1. Use batterboards, string, line level and plumb line to locate footings and piers at deck corners. Dig holes and position piers.

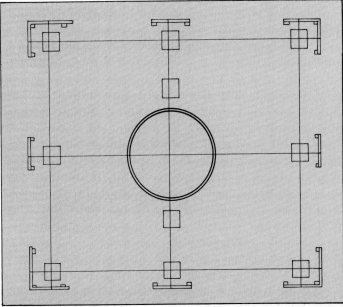

2. With batterboards and leveled string, establish intermediate footing and pier locations. Postion piers in footing holes.

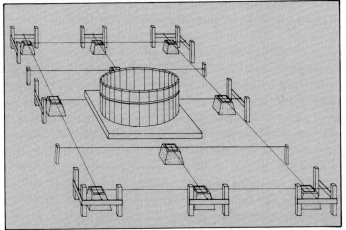

3. Reposition strings so they are 1 inch above pier tops. Level string to make sure all piers are at the same height. Adjust pier height, if necessary, then set piers in concrete.

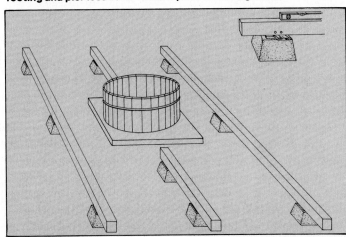

4. Set beams directly on pier blocks. Use a level to check beams at several locations. If beams aren't level, use wood shingles to shim them up, as shown. When beams are level, attach them to piers.

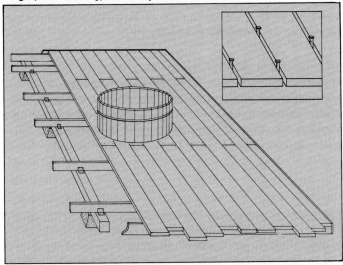

5. Attach joists to beams with the appropriate metal fasteners, then nail decking over joists. Alternate decking board lengths so ends are staggered, as shown. Use 16d nails as spacers between boards, upper right. Spacers are removed once boards are nailed in place.

6. Use a chalk line to mark cutting lines for ends of deck boards. Use a portable circular saw to cut ends flush. Attach headers and fascia boards around perimeter of deck, as shown in the drawing on page 43.

Many states require fencing around spas and hot tubs. Fence should be 5 to 6 feet tall and difficult to climb. Some areas may also require a self-latching gate.

Fences are usually defined as barriers that enclose an area. Garden screens are generally tall, vertical structures—they're often freestanding or come as part of a patio structure. Popular screen materials include lath, bamboo, translucent plastic or glass, and canvas.

Fences and garden screens can act as plant supports. Vines can grow on them or plants can be trained to grow against them. Attach hooks or shelves to the fence or screen to hold plants in containers.

Many states now have laws *requiring* fences and locking gates around outdoor pools to protect children and non-swimmers. These fences usually must be 4 to 5 feet tall and meet certain other requirements. Check with your local building department.

One of the best inexpensive fences is a lattice fence built from lath. One is shown on the following page. Quick-growing vines can be trained to grow on it.

A variation of this is a portable lattice screen. You simply build two or more wood frames, attach latticework to them and hinge the units together, accordion style.

OVERHEAD STRUCTURES

Overheads serve two purposes—to shade the spa or tub and to protect soakers from rain. A solid overhead of

Adjustable bamboo screens on this wooden overhead are raised or lowered as angle of sun changes. Bamboo screens also serve as roof covering.

wood, canvas or corrugated aluminum provides complete protection from sun and rain. Clear glass or plastic keeps rain out and allows a view of the sky. Obscure translucent glass, fiberglass or acrylic plastic provides filtered sunlight. An overhead of wood lath offers partial shade as well as a support for vines. It doesn't keep out rain. Choose overhead materials carefully to get the effect you want.

Redwood lath is a favorite material for vertical screens and overheads. Usually sold by the bundle, lath is relatively inexpensive and easy to work with. Because lath is so lightweight, the structure supporting a lath overhead need not be massive.

If you want only occasional overhead protection, build a frame to support a removable bamboo or canvas shade. The frames should be constructed so the horizontal shades can be rolled back or completely removed as desired. Use either the matchstick or split-reed type of bamboo.

An inexpensive way to provide

Latticework makes an attractive wind and shade screen. This tall screen filters strong afternoon sunlight.

more permanent overhead protection is to frame a bamboo or canvas shade with 1x2s. Build a light frame around the spa or tub to support the panel. The panel can be used horizontally for a flat roof or, if there are two, for a pitched roof.

GAZEBOS

Gazebos provide attractive and practical settings for hot tubs and spas. They shield the unit from weather and afford the user an added measure of privacy. You can either build your own custom gazebo or choose from a number of prefabricated styles.

You'll find prefabricated gazebos in all shapes from octagonal to rectangular or freeform. They'll accommodate most standard shapes of hot tubs and spas.

The gazebo environment is semi-sheltered with filtered light. This provides ideal growing conditions for even the most exotic plant species. Use of the outdoor spa or hot tub is possible beyond normal seasonal limitations because a gazebo offers protection from the elements.

Gazebos are also useful in complying with building codes. Many manufacturers design gazebos to meet state fence and gate requirements for spa installations. That is, they help "child-proof" a spa or tub.

If you have a good view from your property you may not want to obstruct it with a 5-foot fence required by a local building code. A gazebo can be situated to complement the view rather than hinder it. It can also serve as an attractive area divider.

Materials frequently used in construction of prefabricated gazebos are wood, fiberglass, aluminum and heavy steel. Each material has inherent strengths. Woods used for gazebos include redwood, Douglas fir and cedar.

Many steel and aluminum gazebos have a wrought-iron appearance. Climate suitability, material adaptability and appearance are generally the foremost factors in choosing these materials over others.

Gazebos are available in all styles from classic Southern plantation to modern Japanese. Differences in appearance depend on size, materials used, frame and roof variations, and options.

Gazebos usually range in size from 7-1/2-feet to 16-feet square. Many companies offer several sizes of the same model. Some gazebos have decks specifically designed to accommodate standard spa and hot-tub dimensions.

Latticework, stained glass, awning tops and locking doors are options

White lattice overhead suggests a cool retreat for soakers. Latticework is 1x2" lath over a frame of 2x4s.

Redwood gazebo provides shade, privacy and a place to hang plants. Many gazebos come as prefabricated kits.

This glassed-in gazebo can be used day or night in any weather.

used to spruce up many standard models.

Retail prices range from under $1,500 for a 12-foot steel gazebo to $2,500 for the same size unit constructed of clear select redwood. Additions and options increase the cost.

Installation of a gazebo should not pose special problems to homeowners with average building abilities. Kits come with detailed instructions and a list of tools needed for assembly.

FULL ENCLOSURES

Full enclosures for spas and hot tubs are popular because they permit year-round use in any climate. They reduce heating and chemical costs and can offer complete privacy. Many double as indoor-outdoor dining areas, greenhouses or other activity areas.

The advantages of enclosures in cold-weather environments are obvious. They keep the warmth in and the cold out. Windows placed to capture the sun's heat during winter, and the warmth generated by the spa or tub, provide a comfortable indoor climate on cold days.

Full enclosures fall into two categories—*freestanding* and *add-on*. A freestanding enclosure is separate from the house. An add-on is attached to the house. Your family's lifestyle and household routine best determine which style to choose. See page 34.

Add-On Enclosures—Adding a spa or tub room to the house can be more complex and costly than putting a separate enclosure in the yard. Add-ons almost always involve more work.

They should follow the design of the house to avoid looking like an afterthought. Some house designs lend themselves better to add-ons than others.

An add-on enclosure can be convenient—especially in climates where even a short winter walk through the yard is chilling.

Freestanding Enclosures—You have two basic choices in freestanding enclosures: custom-designed built from scratch or prefabricated.

The advantages of designing your own spa or tub room are several. You can match it to the architecture of your house. You can add features not available in most prefab designs, such as a separate room for dressing, showers or a small pool for cooling off after a soak. Freedom in design is limited only by your design abilities and the money you have to spend.

Prefabricated enclosures vary in sophistication, adaptability, cost and construction. Some come with many accessories and options. Others are simple.

Virtually all prefabricated enclosures are of the dome or greenhouse type. Most consist of glass or plastic panels set into wood, metal or plastic frames. One exception is the inflatable dome—air pressure keeps this dome rigid. The rounded shape of a dome sheds snow, ice, wind and rain.

Points To Consider—One effect of enclosing a spa or tub is the "steam-room" atmosphere created. Where comfort is concerned, this added humidity can be beneficial in dry climates, a bane in wet areas.

High humidity also results in water condensation on the enclosure's interior surfaces. Proper ventilation helps keep condensation to a minimum. Ventilation for both prefabricated and custom-designed enclosures is accomplished with air vents, exhaust fans or both. With these features you can achieve almost any temperature and humidity level.

If you're building a conventional enclosure, either freestanding or attached to the house, there are several points to consider. Insulation for walls and ceilings must have a vapor barrier to repel moisture.

Double-glazed windows and skylights are less susceptible to condensation than ordinary ones. Materials for walls, floors and ceilings should be moisture- and decay-resistant. Red-

This large atrium houses pool with an attached spa and has plenty of room for extensive collection of exotic indoor plants. This enclosure is part of original house design.

wood and red cedar are good choices for these surfaces. Left unfinished, these woods absorb excess moisture without damage to the wood. All metal fixtures and hardware, including nails and screws, should be rustproof.

Because of humidity, moisture-loving tropical plants thrive in a spa or tub enclosure. Dome-type enclosures are ideal for ferns. Even the most-fragile varieties flourish because of the even light distribution and tropical-moisture level. White, transparent or translucent materials are best for use in a greenhouse. They do not absorb heat as readily as dark-colored materials. If your spa or tub is in an area where privacy is not a priority, a transparent enclosure with plants can be attractive.

The material you choose for your enclosure will determine how well it stays heated. Opaque surfaces, such as wood, will retain interior heat better than translucent surfaces such as glass and clear plastic. Dark colors absorb more heat than light ones. Dark, opaque surfaces are best in cold climates. They aren't good if you intend to grow plants in the spa or tub enclosure. High heat and lack of natural light make plant growing difficult.

There are many options for people interested in growing plants in an enclosure, such as hanging-basket clips, add-on slat benches for plants, exhaust fans, thermostats, programmed timers for sprinklers and grow lights.

Indoor-outdoor patio leads to outside veranda. Spa is fully protected for year-round use.

Consider potential views when designing a spa or tub enclosure. Large windows give a spacious feeling.

Greenhouse addition around spa provides good light and high humidity for growing plants.

SPA AND TUB COVERS

Most of the reasons for using a cover on a spa or hot tub are obvious. It keeps leaves, debris and children out, keeps heat in and reduces evaporation of water and chemicals.

But there is a new wrinkle you may not be aware of. Many states now offer a tax credit up to 55% on the purchase price of approved solar covers. These covers drastically reduce heating time and sometimes eliminate the need for supplemental heating.

The tax credit is usually subtracted directly from the state income tax you owe—it is not just a deduction. It's not unusual for a solar cover to pay for itself in one season's use. Check tax regulations in your state.

Hot-tub and spa covers may be made of wood, canvas, plastic and fiberglass. Find out which ones qualify for the tax credit if you're in the market for a cover.

Controlling Heat Loss—With or without a cover, overnight heat loss from a swimming pool heated to 82F (28C) is not very significant during the summer. But a spa is smaller and hotter than a swimming pool. It loses heat more rapidly. The best way to minimize this loss is to keep the spa covered whenever it is not in use.

The use of a good-quality bubble-type or foam cover—see next page—will significantly reduce heat loss. If the water surface is exposed to direct sunlight for a good portion of the day, a translucent bubble-type cover works best. The water surface is a good solar energy collector and these covers allow solar energy to pass through while preventing heat loss. If the spa or tub is in the shade, a flexible or solid foam cover is probably best. Depending on thickness, these covers provide greater insulation than bubble-type covers.

Insulating covers not only insulate the water surface from the outside air temperature, they prevent surface heat loss due to wind. Covers also reduce water and chemical evaporation caused by wind and sun.

Foam covers can be used with a rigid cover to increase water heat retention. Rigid covers, like the one shown on the facing page, should be sturdy enough to keep children from getting into the spa or hot tub.

Covers deteriorate rapidly because of the high temperature and chemical content of the average spa or hot tub.

This insulated hot-tub cover controls heat loss, is sturdy enough to keep children out of tub.

To extend the life of the cover, wait at least one hour after adding chlorine before covering the spa or tub.

LIGHTING

If you plan to do any nighttime soaking, you'll need adequate lighting. Careful placement of light fixtures not only creates the desired nighttime mood but is also essential to the safety of soakers.

Indoors, lighting requirements are about the same as for other rooms in the house. Subdued lighting will create a relaxing atmosphere. Just make sure there's enough light for soakers to see their way in and out of the spa or tub. Due to the humidity created by spas and tubs indoors, all light fixtures should be rust-resistant and properly grounded. The circuit should include a GFCI breaker.

Outdoors, both the spa or tub and the path leading to it should be well-lighted, but not over-lighted. Because darkness itself offers a feeling of privacy, you may want lighting to be subtle. Low-level lights along the path will define it without lighting up the rest of the yard. A well-placed spotlight will illuminate the immediate area around the spa or tub, leaving the surrounding area in darkness.

Foam insulating pad efficiently cuts heating costs. It can be used with a cover for even greater savings.

If you plan to use your spa or tub at night, provide adequate lighting. An underwater spa light helps soakers locate spa steps and seating areas.

There is a variety of outdoor light fixtures available. Most outdoor lighting is the energy-saving, low-voltage type.

Besides lighting the area around the spa or tub, you may also want to light up the water. Submersible light fixtures are easy to install in any spa or tub. Some models have a set of colored lenses that can be easily changed to suit the mood of the soaker. For safety, all submersible fixtures should carry UL listing and be installed by a qualified electrician. Use only fixtures specifically made for spa installation.

CHOOSING PLANTS

Plants around the spa or tub make the environment more appealing. Outdoors, screen plantings make the soaker feel less exposed.

When choosing plantings, check with local nurseries to find out which plants grow best in your area. Shrubs and trees that grow well in most parts of the United States include bamboo, Carolina laurel, English laurel, common privet and Pittosporum. All are fast-growing and provide a dense screen.

Always try to leave a little room between fence and decking for vines or other plants. They relieve the starkness of new fences. Creeping fig is a good choice in sun or shade. It will grow close to the fence and needs only occasional trimming. If there's no room between fence and decking, attach hooks to the fence and hang baskets or pots filled with seasonal plants.

Consider planting a grove of trees around your spa or tub. Hot tubs in particular lend themselves to being surrounded by trees. Planting a grove may sound extreme, but even a small lot can handle half a dozen trees planted in a confined area.

If you live in a favorable area, there's nothing as pleasant as a small grove of Coast redwoods. They will create the feeling of bathing in a forest.

Other faster-growing choices for grove trees are Indian laurel, almost any of the eucalyptus species or Monterey pine.

Trees, shrubs or even annuals planted in large containers can make a big difference in the way an outdoor soaking area looks. Use several

Lighting can create a dramatic visual effect. The pool and attached spa shown in the photos at left and below were designed to look best at night.

Potted plants were used to dress up this otherwise bare patio area. More delicate plant varieties can be taken inside during winter months.

different-size containers grouped together, with several varieties of plants.

Both weeping fig and Indian laurel make good container trees. Don't forget to water and fertilize container-grown plants frequently. There's only a limited amount of soil in containers. For best results, don't fill containers with your own garden soil. Buy the best packaged soil mix you can afford.

If you want a contained screen planting, buy or build a box. A good

Another approach is to simply set the spa directly in an existing garden area. A few large planks serve as modest decking for this installation.

size is 20 inches wide by 16 inches deep. Make it whatever length you want the screen to be. Any of the recommended plants work well in this type of container. Such a container can also be adapted for seating.

PROTECTING PLANTS AROUND SPAS AND TUBS

Trees, shrubs, flowering plants and lawns are all natural complements to a spa and hot tub in a home landscape. It's sometimes easy to forget that spa or tub water can adversely affect plants, and vice versa. Here are some points to keep in mind.

Many spa and hot-tub owners want to know if they can use water from a spa or tub on surrounding plantings. The answer is *no*—not if the water has been treated with chlorinating chemicals for more than a few months.

The use of chemicals builds up the amount of *soluble salt* in the water. Excess soluble salt around plants will stunt their growth, burn their foliage or even kill them. Have your local garden center recommend plants that are more salt-tolerant than others.

Most spas and tubs are equipped with a fairly wide deck—2 to 4 feet. The wider the deck, the less neighboring plants will be affected by spa and tub water.

A simple dry well—a 1-foot-wide and 1-1/2-foot-deep trench filled with gravel or stones—placed at the outer edge of the deck will keep spa or tub

One approach is to design a spa into the landscape, rather than design the landscape around the spa. This spa looks natural in its setting.

water from draining directly into planting areas. Don't overlook plants in containers. You may want to use them instead of more permanent plantings.

Container plants around the deck help to relieve the monotony of too much bare space. The containers also provide simple and effective protection from spa and tub water.

PROTECTING SPAS AND TUBS FROM PLANTS

When considering plants for landscaping around spas or tubs, there are several *don'ts*. Don't choose a deciduous tree or shrub—one that drops a lot of leaves. Fruit-bearing trees are also messy. Beware of any tree or shrub that's overly attractive to bees or other annoying insects. All of these can cause accidents around the spa or tub. Don't plant trees that will be too large when they mature. And, don't choose trees or shrubs with extensive root systems. These will cause problems with the unit's plumbing and may eventually ruin a patio surface.

Design Ideas for Spas & Hot Tubs

4

Any location, indoors or out, can serve as a basic foundation for building your spa- or hot-tub environment. The secret is choosing and integrating design elements to enhance the site you've chosen.

The spa and hot-tub installations on the following 16 pages reflect a number of successful design concepts. Look for ideas that can be adapted to your plans. This photo section should inspire creativity and provide solutions to many of your design and landscaping problems.

Contrasting tile colors highlight the artistic geometry of this custom Gunite spa. Its design allows maximum seating area for spa size. Warm tones of used brick help soften the transition from the stylized spa interior to surrounding plantings.

Left: Luxuriant plantings make a cool retreat for a hot soak. Graceful curves of this freeform deck are compatible with the natural garden setting. The overhead is primarily decorative, but it does help define the tub area and lends a visual sense of shelter. The owner also found other uses for the structure, as shown.

Spas & Tubs with a View

If you have a good view from one or more locations in your yard, design the spa or tub to take full advantage of it. A view doesn't have to be panoramic to be pleasant. Careful placement of outdoor screens and plantings can frame an attractive view from the spa or tub, yet provide complete privacy for soaking. Also, blocking an undesirable view is equally as important as preserving a beautiful one.

Below: Multilevel wooden deck serves as a promontory for admiring a magnificent view of desert mountains and city beyond. Redwood decking material and light-blue acrylic spa complement colors of earth and sky. Simple, clean lines of the installation do not compete for viewer's attention.

Above: Privacy is not a problem in wide-open spaces. Above-ground hot tub and flush decking give soakers a broad hilltop view of the surrounding countryside.

Landscaping was kept simple to retain the spacious feeling of this natural desert setting. Privacy screens are usually unnecessary in such sparsely populated areas.

Selective screening was used to block view of tub from closer neighbors while framing a distant view of hillside homes.

Raised seating around tub rim provides a good vantage point for viewing mountains and ocean between soaks. Soakers enter tub by steps located on opposite side. Though tub appears to be perched precariously on the edge of a cliff, it is actually sitting on a sturdy foundation several yards back from the slope. Soil stability should be tested by a soil engineer before attempting an installation like this one.

Hillside Designs

One of the major problems in designing hillside installations is providing enough space around the spa or hot tub for sunbathing, relaxing and other outdoor activities. One way to gain space is to build a hillside deck. The other way is to excavate a level spot in the hillside. Retaining walls are used to terrace the lot into separate levels. This method is also preferable if you want planting areas in the yard.

Space for this spa was actually carved out of a hillside. Walls and ceiling were formed with reinforced concrete and rough-textured with stucco. Natural rock pillars at entrance give you the feeling of soaking in a grotto.

This owner found terracing a practical solution to gain space in a narrow, hillside yard. If the spa were at pool level, the retaining wall behind it would have to be much taller. This would cut off sunlight to the spa and make the yard look smaller. Additional space was gained by allowing upper-level deck to overhang pool 2 feet.

Pool and spa are at same level on this hillside lot. Wooden deck provides additional level space beyond the pool. A retaining wall creates level space for spa and pool, and provides a gentle slope above for hillside plantings.

Working with Nature

Few real hot springs offer all the advantages of a man-made spa. Yet, the spas shown here look as though they were designed by Mother Nature. The key to simulating a natural spring is the careful selection and placement of rocks, earth and plantings. Use plants and rocks native to the surroundings. An alpine pool, for instance, would not be found in a desert landscape. Also, you would not find a natural spring cropping up in the middle of a concrete patio. These spas look best as part of an overall natural-landscaping scheme.

This spa looks as though it were carved out of a natural rock outcropping on this hillside lot. The 'rock' is actually precast, textured concrete, but it would take an extremely close inspection to tell the difference.

Heavy plantings simulate the dense undergrowth found in a coastal forest. Large boulders around spa add realism to the scene. Many plants are native to the area. Compatible cultivated plants were introduced for color.

What Goes Overhead

The most common reason for building an overhead structure is to provide shade while retaining a sense of openess. Some overheads are more decorative than functional, but they do have other uses. They can provide support for climbing vines or be used for hanging potted plants and decorations.

Overheads can be freestanding or attached to the house. Solid overheads provide full shade and protection from rain and snow.

Lath and spaced-board overheads give partial shade while imparting an open feeling. For more information on designing spa and tub overheads, see pages 46-48.

Closely spaced lath on this gazebo-style overhead provides partial shade for above-ground spa. Design makes overhead and spa look like a single structure.

Solid patio overhead shades spa portion of swimming pool. Spa receives full sunlight during morning hours, full shade in afternoon.

Lattice overhead and vertical screen are incorporated into one structure. Circular "windows" create sunny areas on deck for sunbathing.

Large, ornate patio roof shades both spa and large brick patio in background. It also serves as a second-story veranda.

Indoor Spas & Tubs

If you want a spa or hot tub indoors, you have two options. You can either remodel an existing room in the house or add on a spa or tub room. In most cases, adding a room gives you more control over design and location.

If you already have enough room in your house for a spa or hot tub, you may be able to save money by remodeling an existing room. The first question you must ask is, "How will I get the spa or hot tub inside the room?" Many people don't think about this task and are surprised at the cost and work involved in doing it.

Notice that all these indoor installations have plenty of light. Plan for spacious windows and adequate night-lighting. For more information on indoor spas and tubs, see pages 33-34.

Top Right: The walls in this room consist of a series of sliding glass doors. When doors are open, there is enough cross-ventilation to easily dispel excess humidity created by spa. Right: Providing adequate air circulation around a wooden tub is important. Here, the tub is actually resting on the ground outside the house. The room was built over it so the floor is flush with the tub rim.

This spacious screened-in patio can hardly be called an indoor room. It does meet the requirements of being a fully enclosed structure added on to the house. The owners built it to provide filtered sunlight and to keep bugs out.

Wooden floor and paneling are used to absorb excess moisture in this spa-room addition. Both redwood and red cedar will do this without damage to the wood. Exhaust fan above windows vents excess humidity to outdoors.

Glass porch enclosure makes an excellent greenhouse for plants. Plan for adequate ventilation in greenhouse-type enclosures. They can get unbearably hot during summer months. Cooling will be needed in some hot climates.

Spas & Swimming Pools

Spas and pools naturally go together. They can share the same support equipment—pump, heater and filter—and the same water. As these photos show, spas can be attached to the pool by means of a water channel, or be designed right into the pool itself. For more information on spas attached to swimming pools, see page 13.

This is the most conventional way to add a spa to an existing pool. A concrete dam separates the spa area from the main pool. A small channel allows filtered, chemically treated pool water to enter the spa. Hot water for the spa enters through hydrojets. Spa has a separate drain.

Soakers have to do some wading to use this spa. Underwater bridge from pool edge to spa allows access through ankle-deep water.

Raising the spa's water level above that of the pool creates visual depth. Retainer wall behind spa creates stepped effect.

Spa shape continues lines of curved steps leading to this free-form pool.

Red tile against bare concrete decking and glass-smooth water create a dramatic scene. Spa tile is repeated around pool waterline. This spa is shown from another angle on the title page.

Designs in Wood

Wood is a natural material for building decking, steps and other structures around hot tubs. Many of the hot-tub installations shown in this book exemplify the creative uses of wood. But wood can also enhance the appearance of a spa, as shown here. From decks to screens to overheads, wood imparts a warm, natural feeling to any installation. For more information on wooden structures for spas and tubs, see pages 40-49.

This light-blue fiberglass spa stands in sharp contrast to the redwood deck.

Wooden decking was carefully cut and fitted to complement the unusual shape of this fiberglass spa. Deck, overhead, lattice screen and railing form a completely integrated structure.

This installation shows many of the ways wood can be used around a spa or tub. Low wooden borders separate plank walkway from planting areas. Latticework extends height of standard 6-foot board fence to provide privacy for raised tub area.

Modest decking provides just enough room to sit around outside of spa. Dark-brown spa and wooden deck fit naturally into this garden area.

Designs in Masonry

The word 'masonry' encompasses perhaps the broadest range of building materials known. From natural stone to glazed tile, each category offers an endless selection of shapes, sizes, colors and patterns.

Because concrete and Gunite spas are themselves masonry, they're adaptable to practically any masonry material. But masonry is by no means limited to these spas. The warm earth tones of brick and adobe patio tiles provide an excellent setting for a wooden hot tub. Bricks, tile or textured concrete around the rim of a fiberglass spa give it a solid, built-in appearance. For more information on designing with masonry, see pages 36-40.

Angled sides give this spa a sturdy, massive look. Design may have been inspired by early Aztec architecture. Unglazed tiles are slip-resistant.

Raised brick decking around this concrete spa offers ample room for seating, displaying potted plants.

Precast concrete blocks and round steppingstones combine with natural creek stones to make a simple but attractive installation. Materials are relatively inexpensive and the work is easily done by the average do-it-yourselfer.

Concrete patio around this spa is surfaced with a porous masonry material that goes under the trade name of *Kool Decking*. This non-slip surface is cooler on the feet than ordinary concrete. Stucco wall is just tall enough to define patio area.

Cool Pools

If you don't have a swimming pool, cold shower or natural stream next to your spa or tub, consider installing a cool pool. Many soakers enjoy the bracing feeling they get when plunging into cold water after a hot soak.

Cool pools can use the same pump and filtration system as the spa or tub. The equipment must be plumbed so water bypasses the heater when diverted to the cool pool.

Wine-vat cool pool is just large enough for a cold dunk after soaking in the tub. Small cool pools like this can be hooked into the tub's support equipment, or simply drained and refilled at periodic intervals.

Dual spas offer soakers the option of hot or cold hydrotherapy. Special support equipment is required to operate two spas of this size.

Plantings

Though planting around the spa or tub is one of the last things you do, it should be one of the first things you plan. In the initial planning stages, determine how you'll integrate plants and structures into the overall landscape design. For more information on planting around spas and tubs, see pages 54-57.

Top Left: Bamboo, ferns and potted begonias add a tropical touch to this hot-tub retreat. Plantings are in scale with massive timbers used for decking and fence. **Left:** Plants in containers relieve the stark appearance of a new installation. Use them for color until permanent plantings mature.

Flowering vines such as crape myrtle at right are not only colorful, but make good privacy screens. Don't plant vines like this too close to spa or tub—flower petals can be messy.

Use trees and shrubs to break up large expanses of masonry. Here, plantings help reduce reflective glare from light-colored stucco wall.

Air blowers force air through holes in the floor and seat areas of a spa, or through a bubbler ring in the bottom of a hot tub. The increased water turbulence gives bathers an overall massage effect.

You'll need *support equipment* to heat, circulate and filter water in a spa or hot tub. Support equipment can be purchased separately or as a package, usually called a *skid pack*.

Support equipment consists of *pump, filter, heater, air blower* and necessary plumbing and hardware.

The pump circulates water through the system. It usually powers hydrotherapy jets, commonly called *hydrojets*. The filter helps keep the water

Left: Selecting the right support equipment assures best performance from your spa or hot tub. An experienced dealer can help you properly match components.

clean by removing minute particles of dirt, debris and algae. The heater heats the water to the desired temperature. The air blower agitates the water with forced air that comes out of tiny holes in the bottom of the spa or from a *bubbler ring* in a hot tub. Bubbles created by forced air provide bathers with a massage effect.

SKID PACK OR INDIVIDUAL COMPONENTS?

Skid packs consist of matched components for various-sized spas and tubs. Individual components are

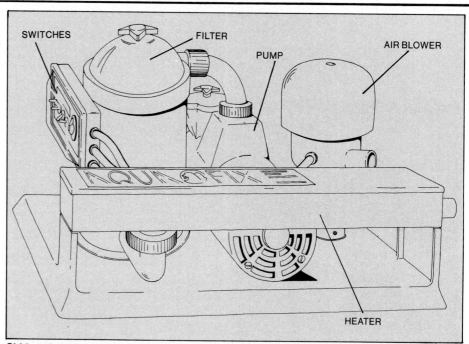

Skid packs take much of the work out of choosing and installing support equipment. Most, however, are designed for smaller spa and tub installations.

Pump detail shows location of strainer basket and housing. The basket keeps leaves and other debris from clogging the pump mechanism.

Skid packs like this usually come preplumbed, ready to install. This one is installed on a portable spa. It includes pump, filter, electric heater and air blower.

sometimes used for large spas or for spas that share support equipment with a swimming pool.

SKID PACKS

Before the advent of skid packs, consumers had to select individual components for the support system. They often picked wrong-size, poorly matched components. When the owner or installer put them together, the result was often a mess.

Then came the skid pack. Its chief advantage was that all components were electrically and hydraulically matched. There now is a pack to fit most spas and tubs.

Skid packs are usually factory-tested, which minimizes the risk of on-site problems. They generally cost more than the same parts purchased individually, but consumers are as-

Pump Detail

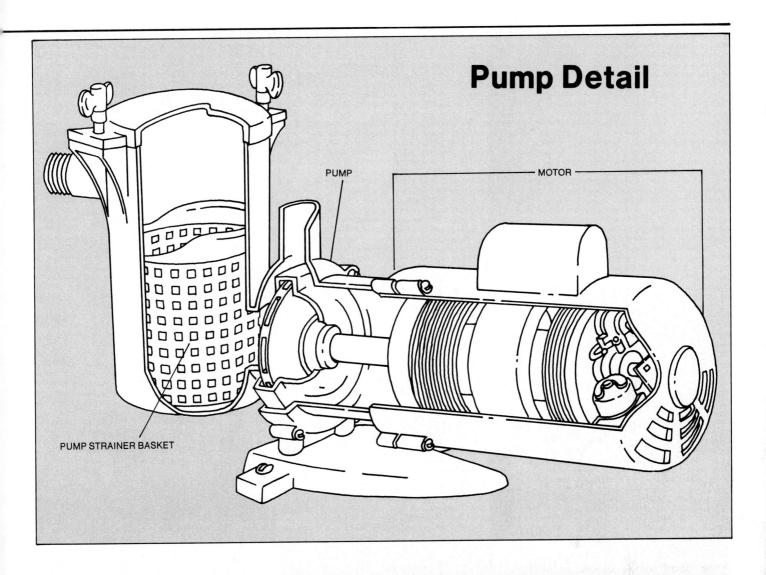

PUMP

MOTOR

PUMP STRAINER BASKET

sured of getting a smoothly functioning system.

Preplumbed skid packs are easy to install. Most skid packs consist of a pump, filter, and electric heater. On these, two simple lines must be connected from the equipment at the spa or hot tub. A suction line draws water from the spa or tub. A return line puts water back in. If the skid pack comes with an air blower, a third line carries air to the air bubbler in the spa or a bubbler ring in the hot tub.

INDIVIDUAL COMPONENTS

Most skid packs are designed for smaller-size spas and tubs. For large, heavily used units, a separate pump, filter and heater may be needed to handle the load.

Choosing individual units provides flexibility. Instead of being locked into a particular system, the user can later add larger individual components.

Two-speed pump operates at low speed for water filtration and heating, at high speed to operate hydrojets. Two-speed switch is located on the pump motor at left.

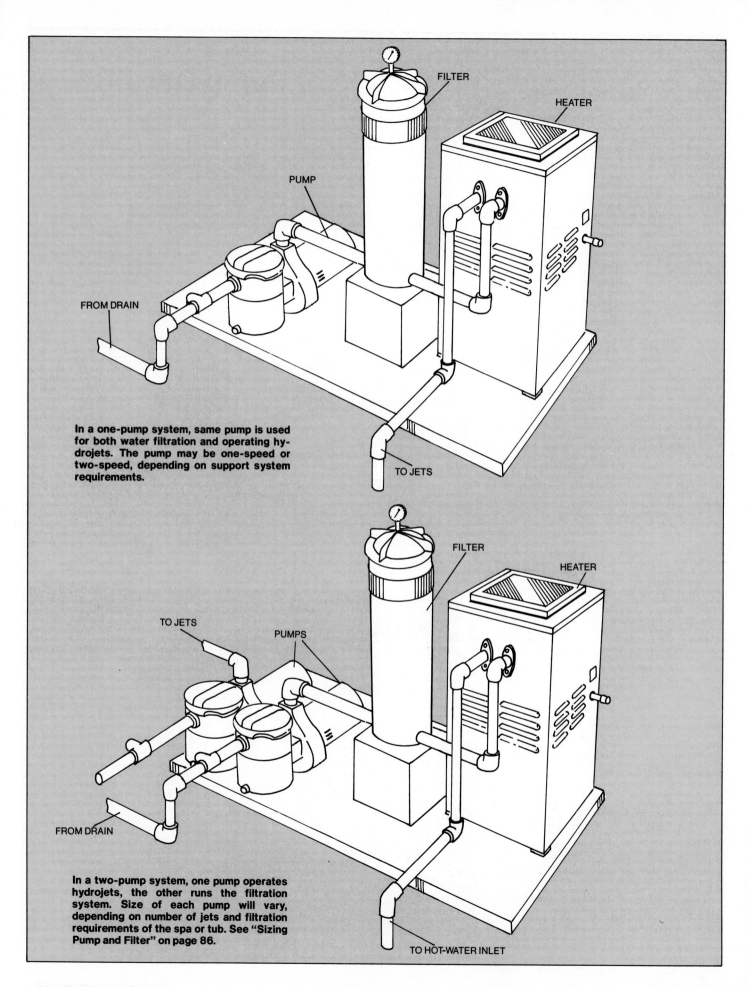

FILTER

HEATER

PUMP

FROM DRAIN

TO JETS

In a one-pump system, same pump is used for both water filtration and operating hydrojets. The pump may be one-speed or two-speed, depending on support system requirements.

FILTER

HEATER

TO JETS

PUMPS

FROM DRAIN

In a two-pump system, one pump operates hydrojets, the other runs the filtration system. Size of each pump will vary, depending on number of jets and filtration requirements of the spa or tub. See "Sizing Pump and Filter" on page 86.

TO HOT-WATER INLET

Time clock automatically runs pump for filtration. It can be set for any length of time during a 24-hour period. Clock is usually installed at support equipment location.

KNOW YOUR EQUIPMENT

Whether you decide to buy a skid pack or individual components, the following information should be useful. It will help you match appropriate equipment with the spa or hot tub you choose.

PUMPS

Water in a spa or tub is seldom completely replaced with fresh water. To stay clean and hot, the water must circulate through a filter and heater.

The device used most often to move water through the system is a 3/4-HP to 2-HP centrifugal pump. The larger the spa or tub, the more powerful the pump must be. Pump size also depends on what it's being used for. A pump used only to circulate water for filtration and heating needn't be as large as one that also operates hydrojets.

Diameter of pipes used in plumbing, number of hydrojets, plumbing configuration and where the support equipment is placed also affect pump size.

Spas and hot tubs can be fitted with a one-speed pump, two pumps, or a two-speed pump. Most spas are fitted with the more energy-efficient two-speed pump. In the two-pump system, one pump is driven by a low horsepower motor for circulation and heating. The other is driven by a larger motor for operating the hydrojets.

In a two-speed, one-pump system, the motor runs at high speed, approximately 3,500 rpm, to provide hydrojet action. When the jets aren't in use,

All filters for spas and tubs should have a water-pressure gage. A change in water pressure indicates the filter needs cleaning.

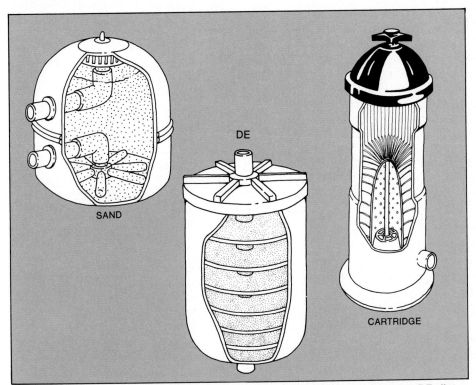

SAND

DE

CARTRIDGE

Cartridge filters are most often used for family-size spas and hot tubs. Sand and DE, diatomaceous earth, filters are used for unusually large spas or for spa swimming-pool combinations.

Reusable filter elements for cartridge filters are easily removed and cleaned with a garden hose. Regular cleaning extends cartridge life.

fine as DE or sand, but they do provide good-quality water with minimum maintenance. Almost 95% of all spa and tub installations use cartridge filters. The remaining 5% use DE or sand filters.

Some installers prefer DE filters because they're more efficient than cartridge filters, especially for larger spas and tubs. But cleaning and servicing these filters is somewhat more difficult. When a DE filter reaches its maximum holding capacity, it must be reverse-flow backwashed or manually cleaned. Many swimming-pool owners are familiar with this process.

After the filter has been backwashed, a new coating of DE must be added before starting a new filter cycle. DE filters are favored in commercial installations, such as public spas, because they can carry a heavier dirt load than cartridge filters.

Sand filters use a uniform grade of hard surface silica as a filtering material. Sand filters are cleaned with the reverse-flow backwash process.

In the backwash process, DE and sand filters use some of the filtered and chemically treated spa or tub water to clean the filter material. It's then discharged as waste water. If selecting one of these filters for your unit, take into account the amount of spa or tub water lost with each backwashing. Also note how various filter systems handle waste-water disposal. Your dealer can explain the cleaning operation necessary for the filter equipment you choose.

Correct sizing of the pump and filter is important to the successful operation of any spa or hot tub. The filter must be large enough to clean the amount of water pumped through it. If the pump is too large, water flows through the filter too fast and the filter can't operate efficiently. For more information, see "Sizing the Equipment," page 86.

WATER PURIFICATION SYSTEMS

Some spa and hot-tub owners use another water-cleaning component in addition to a filter. This is a purification system that automatically keeps the water free of microorganisms without using chemicals.

There are at least four such systems on the market. Although these units do purify water, some experts in the spa and tub industry warn against

the pump kicks back to a lower speed to circulate water through the jets for heating and filtering only.

Pumps are made of brass and bronze, or different types of plastic. Plastic pumps are the most widely used for home installations. Overall, plastic pumps have proven trustworthy in other applications, such as dishwashers, for more than 20 years.

Plastic pumps differ in durability and price—quality models usually use more-durable plastics. One widely used, durable plastic for pumps goes under the trade name of *Noryl*.

FILTERS

A filter removes solid residue, algae and dirt from the water. Different types of filters, such as diatomaceous earth, called DE filters, sand filters and cartridge filters use different material to collect particles.

A cartridge filter has a reusable cartridge of non-woven polyester, Dacron or similar material. Cartridges require periodic cleaning with water. The filtering materials used aren't as using them *instead* of regular chemical purification.

Except for the chlorine generator described below, these systems offer no *residual* germ-killing action. In other words, the water must be pumped through the support system to be purified. The units do not *immediately* kill microorganisms that enter the water while soakers are using the spa or tub. Residual germ-killing action is necessary to protect soakers if more than one is using the spa or tub at a time. Only chemical treatment does this. Generally, these systems should be viewed only as backups for regular chemical purification.

Ultraviolet Water Sterilizers— Shortwave ultraviolet energy, called UV energy, causes the *protoplasm*, or cell content, of microorganisms to explode. Bacteria, algae, viruses and other microscopic bodies can be killed in this fashion.

To adapt this method to spa and hot tub use, protective coatings or encasements for the UV bulb are necessary. One company has patented a process that encases UV tubes in practically indestructible fluoropolymer sleeves. The protected tubes are then placed inside a circulating water unit, and the UV exposure kills microorganisms.

Unlike chemical treatment, UV sterilization doesn't alter the composition of water or affect its odor or taste. In most cases, operation for a few hours a day will sanitize all the water in an average-size spa or tub. One manufacturer claims these sterilizers use about as much electricity as a 150-watt light bulb.

Ionizers—Electrical currents running through metal electrodes produce ions that kill bacteria and algae. One system uses copper and silver electrodes located in the water inlet pipe to the spa or tub. Harmful organisms are killed and then removed by a filter.

Chlorine Generators—Chlorine generators manufacture pure, *nascent chlorine.* Nascent chlorine is odorless, long-lasting and kills all waterborne bacteria. The amount of solution in the water can be measured by an ordinary water test kit. See page 147.

Ozone Generators—Ozone is the most powerful oxidant known to man. It sterilizes water by reducing organic chemicals to their major elements of carbon dioxide and water.

Ozone generators, or *ozonators,* de-signed for spas and hot tubs convert oxygen in the air to ozone and infuse it into the water. The disinfected water is then suctioned back into the spa or tub. Ozone disinfection is approximately 60 times faster than chemical purification. Power consumption is minimal.

HEATERS

Most heaters used for spas and hot tubs are either *fossil-fueled* or *electric.* Most fossil-fueled heaters are designed to use natural gas or propane. Several manufacturers make fossil-fueled spa and pool heaters that use fuel oil. *Solar* heating systems are also becoming popular as a primary or supplemental source of hot water. These systems usually rely on one of the other two types for backup heating during cloudy weather. For a discussion on solar heating for spas and tubs, see page 97.

For those with an ample wood supply, there are several models of wood-fired water heaters available. Adapting these to spa and tub support

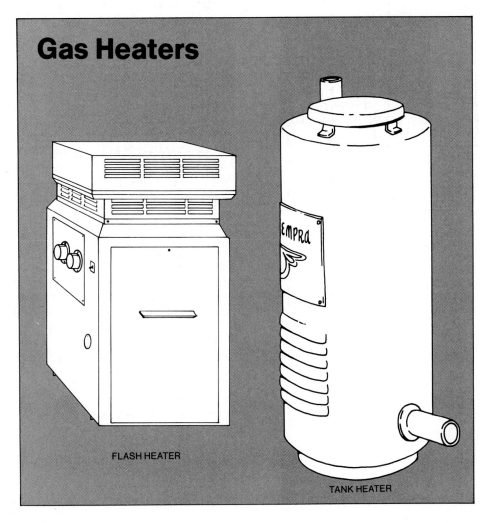

Gas Heaters

FLASH HEATER

TANK HEATER

Many dealers offer matched pipes and fittings for preplumbing spas and hot tubs.

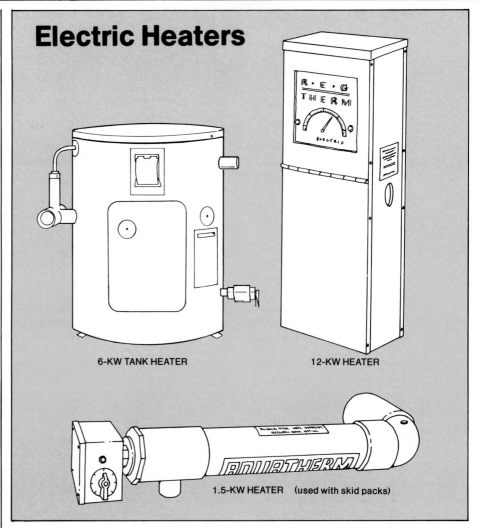

Electric Heaters

6-KW TANK HEATER

12-KW HEATER

1.5-KW HEATER   (used with skid packs)

systems usually requires the services of a professional installer. Wood-stove dealers can provide information on wood-fired water heaters and recommend local installers. You'll find wood-stove dealers in the Yellow Pages under "Stoves, wood, coal, etc."

The prime factors in choosing a heater are relative energy costs in your area and the energy efficiency of the heater you buy. To help compare actual heating costs, see pages 89-90. Another point to consider is the *rate* at which different heater types heat water. You may want to spend a bit more for a unit that heats your spa or tub more quickly. Different heater types are discussed here.

Fossil-Fueled Heaters—Almost all fossil-fueled spa, tub and pool heaters are atmospheric burners, also called *flash heaters.* Air is pulled into the burner while fuel—such as natural gas, propane, or fuel oil—enters through an orifice. The air-and-fuel mixture makes a large, open flame to heat a heat exchanger, which is usually one or more copper tubes. Fins on the tubes provide fast heat transfer to the water flowing through them. Water flow rate depends on tube diameter and pump size.

These heaters are highly efficient. They're designed to heat water on demand and maintain desired temperature while the spa or tub is in use.

A larger-size gas heater will heat water more quickly than a small one. Both use the *same amount of fuel* to bring water to the desired temperature. Consider using a larger heater if heat will be turned off between uses. For more information on heater sizing, see page 88.

Another type of fossil-fueled water heater is the *tank heater.* This uses a small, open flame to heat a large body of water. Home water heaters are of this type. Tank heaters are rarely used for spas and hot tubs because of the slow recovery period.

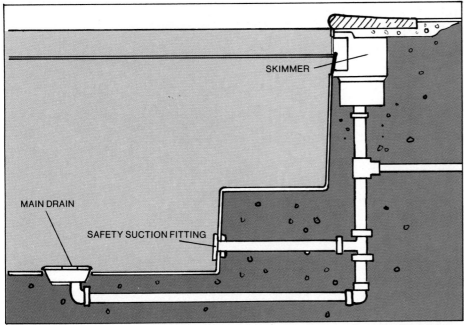

A second drain, called a *safety suction fitting,* should be installed on all spas and hot tubs.

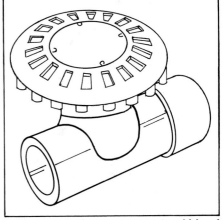

Anti-vortex drain cover prevents whirlpool effect caused by drain suction.

Electric Heaters—These heaters are most often integrated into skid packs for smaller spa and tub installations. They also come as standard equipment on most portable spas.

Their heat output is somewhat less than most fossil-fueled heaters. Also, electric heaters raise water temperature more slowly than fossil-fueled heaters. Because of the long heatup time required, electric heaters are most efficient when maintaining a steady temperature in the spa. For this reason, spas and tubs with electric heaters are usually kept heated at all times if they're used more than occasionally.

An electric heater's ability to maintain a stable water temperature depends on its size. Most manufacturers offer 1.5, 6 and 12-kilowatt heaters. The 1.5 and 6-kilowatt models are used for spas and tubs of 300 gallons or less, the 12-kilowatt model for units holding up to 500 gallons of water. Most electric heaters are wired for 220-volt systems.

Electric heaters cost less to buy than fossil-fueled heaters. They make good backup heaters for solar heating systems—solar heats the spa or tub during the day and the electric heater maintains the heat during evening hours.

PLUMBING AND FITTINGS

Selecting the right-size pipes and fittings is important when designing a spa or hot-tub system. Several factors influence pipe diameter. You'll need to know:

- Flow rate of water measured in gallons per minute.
- Efficiency of the pump system in relation to resistance in the plumbing.
- Length of pipe.
- Number of fittings and angles.

Each hydrojet and return-inlet fitting has a minimum flow requirement. Too many elbows, tees or fittings will reduce the water action in your spa or tub. Most standard installations use 1-1/2-inch diameter pipes and fittings. To take the guesswork out of sizing, some manufacturers offer plumbing kits with matched components.

DRAINS AND SUCTION FITTINGS

For safety, spas and tubs should have two water-return outlets. Too much suction in one drain can cause a person's hair to get entangled in the drain fitting.

Spas with floor drains should have a second drain, called a *safety suction fitting,* on one of the side walls. The suction fitting is connected to the main drain line. Spas and hot tubs with side drains should also have a safety suction fitting in the wall, at least 12 inches away from the main drain.

Drains should have covers, called *anti-vortex covers.* These help break up the whirlpool effect caused by drain

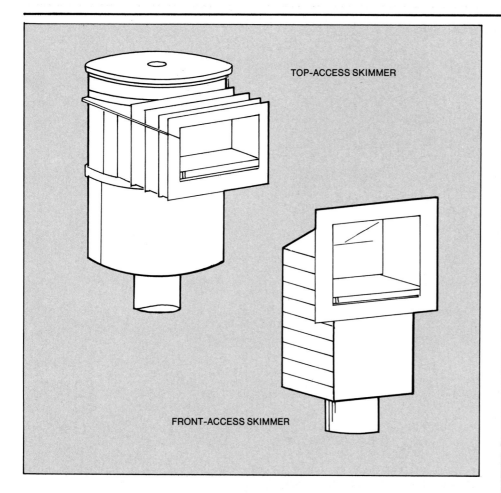

TOP-ACCESS SKIMMER

FRONT-ACCESS SKIMMER

Top-access skimmers are so-called because leaf basket is removed from the top.

On front-access skimmer, leaf basket is removed from the skimmer inlet opening in the spa or tub.

suction. On some spas, the drain consists of a series of small holes spread out across the floor of the unit. The drain holes evenly distribute the suction, so no one drain hole has enough force to pull hair into it.

SKIMMERS

A skimmer is perhaps the most necessary piece of optional equipment you can buy for your spa or tub. It skims leaves and other debris off the water surface, preventing clogged drains and plumbing.

There are two types of skimmers for spas: top-access and front-access. On top-access skimmers, the leaf basket is removed from the top; on front-access skimmers, from the front. The advantage of front-access skimmers is that they can be covered with a decking surface.

Hot tubs require a special type of

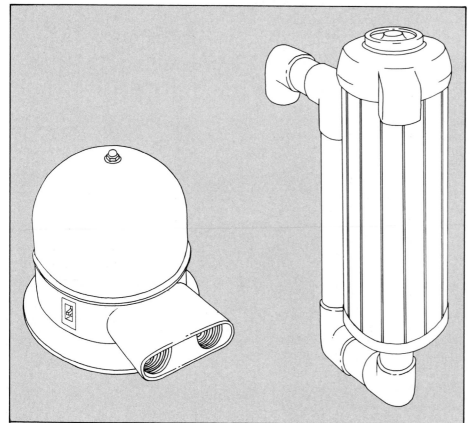

Air blowers come in many shapes and sizes. They're used to operate air bubblers in spas and tubs.

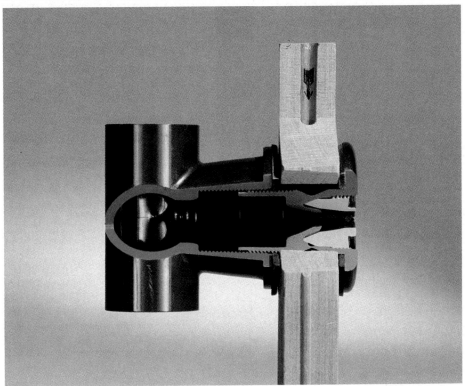

Hydrojets operate on the venturi principle, much like the carburetor on a gasoline engine.

skimmer. These are long and narrow and fit vertically on one of the tub staves.

AIR BLOWERS

According to veterans in the spa business, the first air blowers were vacuum cleaners operated in reverse. The object was to agitate the water without using hydrojets and larger pumps. Users found that air bubbles felt good and were as much fun as jets.

Eventually, the "vacuum cleaners" were replaced by air blowers specifically designed to match the requirements of various-size spas and tubs.

As fiberglass spas became popular, manufacturers incorporated air channels for blowers into the spa design. Today, almost all fiberglass spas come with built-in air channels.

Motors—One type of motor currently used to drive blowers is a *flow-through* unit. The air is pulled through the opening in the fan assembly and discharged through and around the motor itself. Air pumped is the same air that cools the motor. Unfortunately, flow-through motors are prone to overheating and damage from water.

One manufacturer offers a line of blowers with *bypass* motors. Air is pulled in through the fan assembly and discharged peripherally, out the side of the fan assembly. The motor has its own separate cooling fan.

The bypass motor was developed specifically for use in spas and hot tubs. It's expensive but it offers features flow-through motors can't match. The bypass motor is safer because it's not as susceptible to overheating or water damage. Performance is superior to that of flow-through motors.

When you're comparison shopping, be sure to ask which type of air-blower motor comes with the spa or tub.

Jet fitting for a hot tub.

HYDROJETS

A hydrojet works by pumping water under pressure through an orifice. This creates a vacuum that pulls in air and mixes it with water, producing an agitating effect. As water flow and pressure increase, more air is drawn through the jet, resulting in more water agitation.

In some systems, an air blower is used to increase hydrojet action by injecting air into the vacuum line. This practice is not recommended. If a spa user blocks one of the jets, water can be forced through the air line into the blower, ruining it.

SIZING EQUIPMENT

Selecting and combining appropriate equipment is the key to good spa or tub operation. The charts and equations on the following pages demonstrate how to match components for maximum efficiency and minimum utility costs.

SIZING PUMP AND FILTER

First size the pump, then match the filter to the pump. The pump must be powerful enough to operate the hydrojets in your spa or tub and provide adequate circulation for filtering the water. The filter must have the capacity to filter the water being pumped through it.

There are a number of variables involved in selecting the right-size pump and filter for your spa or tub. Kind and number of hydrojets, water volume in the spa or tub and back-pressure in the plumbing system must all be considered.

The best way to size the pump and filter is to take your plans to a qualified dealer or installer. Provide him with as much information on your installation as possible. Include the kind and number of hydrojets in the spa or tub, water volume and distance between the unit and the support-equipment site.

The first step in sizing the pump is to match it to the number of jets in the system. To operate efficiently, most hydrojets need 12 to 15 gallons of water pumped through them per minute. Thus, if your spa or tub has 4 jets, you'll need a pump that delivers 50 gallons to 60 gallons per minute. In most systems, a 1-HP pump will meet these requirements.

A general rule for matching pumps to hydrojets is that each jet requires 1/4 horsepower. This rule applies to most spa and tub installations where the distance between the spa or tub and the pump does not exceed 20 feet. Thus a 1/2-HP pump will operate 2 jets, a 3/4-HP pump will operate 3 jets, and so forth.

In addition to hydrojet operation, the pump must be sized for adequate filtration. Generally, all of the water in a spa or tub should be completely cycled through the filter at least twice per hour. Most pumps sized to operate two or more hydrojets in a spa or tub up to 600 gallons will easily do this. For example, in a 500-gallon spa or tub, a 1-HP pump can completely cycle all the water through the filter in less than 10 minutes. The time required to cycle the total water volume through the filter is called the *turnover rate*.

To size a pump for filtration, divide the total water volume in the spa or tub by the desired turnover rate. This gives you the required pump *flow rate*, expressed in gallons per minute. The turnover rate for most systems is anywhere from 10 to 30 minutes.

Usually, the flow rate needed for filtration is somewhat less than for operating hydrojets. In a two-pump system, the larger pump is matched to the jets and the smaller pump is sized for filtration only. In this system, a 1/4-HP pump is usually adequate for

Pump sizes for spas and hot tubs range from 2HP left down to 1/6HP right.

Spas with two or more hydrojets require proper matching of jets to pump.

Replaceable cartridges come in different sizes to match filter shape and capacity.

filtering spas and tubs up to 600 gallons.

In a one-pump system, a pump sized to operate hydrojets may deliver too much water through the filter for proper filtration. In this case, a bypass must be installed to divert some of the water past the filter when the jets are on. Some filters come with a built-in bypass pipe for this purpose. If the system has a two-speed pump, match the higher speed rating to the jets, the lower speed to filtration.

The most difficult part of sizing a pump comes in determining what its actual flow rate will be once it's hooked into the system. The flow rate of any given pump is affected by back-pressure in the plumbing system. The higher the back-pressure, the fewer gallons per minute the pump can cycle.

The amount of water back-pressure, expressed in pounds per square inch, or *psi*, depends on the amount of flow restriction, or *head loss*, in the plumbing. Head loss, expressed in feet, is affected by pipe diameter, length of pipe runs and number of elbows and other fittings in the plumbing. Plumbing systems for most residential spas and tubs have head losses of 50 feet to 60 feet.

Pump manufacturers supply performance charts with their pumps. These show how many gallons different-size pumps can deliver against different back-pressures or head losses.

Check with a qualified dealer or installer to see if you need to compute the head loss in your spa or tub plumbing. In most cases, the dealer or installer has worked with numerous installations and can choose the right-size pump based on your installation plans. If you need to determine head loss or back-pressure, have the dealer or installer help you with your computations. Then refer to pump manufacturer's performance charts to choose the right-size pump.

Filter Capacity— Once you've sized the pump, matching the filter is easy. Simply match the filter capacity, in gallons per minute, to the flow rate of the pump.

Filters are often sized by the number of square feet of filter surface contained within the filter housing. The amount of water each square foot of filter can cycle, times the total number of square feet of filter will determine the overall filter capacity.

Most manufacturers rate cartridge filters at 1 gallon per minute per foot of filter surface. So a 50-square-foot

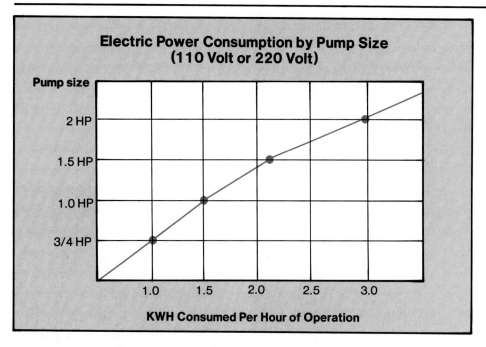

Electric Power Consumption by Pump Size (110 Volt or 220 Volt)

Pump size

- 2 HP
- 1.5 HP
- 1.0 HP
- 3/4 HP

KWH Consumed Per Hour of Operation: 1.0, 1.5, 2.0, 2.5, 3.0

filter will cycle 50 gallons per minute. DE filters are rated at 2 gallons per minute per square foot. High-rate sand filters are rated at 20 gallons to 22 gallons per minute per square foot.

With cartridge filters, it's better to oversize them slightly, than to undersize them. If a 50-gpm cartridge filter is working at full capacity, it must be cleaned about once a month. If the same filter is cycling 40 gallons per minute it may need cleaning only once every two months. There are practical limits to sizing filters, both in initial cost and filtering efficiency.

PUMP POWER CONSUMPTION

Pump power consumption can be computed from the above table. Gallons per minute climb with pump horsepower. So does energy consumption. For maximum efficiency, size the pump accurately. Pumps of 2 HP or more should use 220-volt motors.

You can accurately gage the cost of pump operation using the current kilowatt hour, or kwh, rate for your area. For example, at 7 cents per kwh, to filter the water of a 500-gallon spa for one hour with a 3/4-HP pump would cost about 8 cents. When computing pump-operation costs, include anticipated time pump will be operating hydrojets. Multiply the daily cost by 30 to get estimated monthly cost of pump operation.

HEATER SIZE

There are two reasons for choosing the right-size heater. First, the heater must be large enough to heat the water quickly and maintain it at the desired temperature. It shouldn't run constantly to do its job. This leads to the second reason: Proper sizing ensures maximum energy efficiency. If a heater is too large or too small, it won't operate at peak efficiency.

How They're Sized—Spa, tub and pool heaters are sized by the amount of heat they produce. The amount is measured in British Thermal Units, or *Btu,* generated per hour. One Btu equals the amount of heat necessary to raise one pound of water one degree Fahrenheit.

Fossil-fueled heaters have an *input* rating and an *output* rating.

Both are expressed in Btu per hour. The input rating is the total amount of heat produced from the heater's flame. The output rating is the amount of heat that actually contributes to heating the water. From the input and output ratings, you can determine the *heating efficiency* of the unit you're buying. Most fossil-fueled water heaters are 70% to 80% efficient.

When sizing the heater to a spa or tub, you'll be using the *output rating.* When determining heating costs, you'll be using the *input rating.* Both ratings should appear on a metal rating tag affixed to the unit. If only one figure appears, ask the dealer which rating it represents. Most heater manufacturers provide sizing charts with their heaters. These usually show how much time it takes various-size heaters to raise the water temperature a given number of degrees. The charts generally show the heater input rating only.

Electric water heaters are virtually 100% efficient—all the heat produced by the burner is used to heat the water. On these units, input equals output so one Btu rating is given.

How To Figure—The area method is probably the most accurate for heater sizing. It's used by the majority of heater manufacturers. With this method, you can determine the *minimum* output necessary to maintain the desired temperature in your spa or tub. Unless you keep the water heated continuously, choose a heater with an output greater than the minimum requirement. Size will depend on how fast you want the water.

To use this method you need to determine these factors:
- Water surface area of the spa in square feet.
- Temperature desired.
- For outdoor units, the average outdoor temperature of the coldest month during which the spa is to be used. Call your local weather bureau for this information.
- For indoor units, the average room temperature.

Then, determine the difference between desired spa water temperature and outside air temperature. For example, if desired water temperature is 102F (39C) and the average outside temperature is 65F (18C), then the desired water temperature rise is 37F (3C).

To determine necessary heater output in Btu, use the following formula. The number 12 in the formula represents water-surface heat loss. Each square foot of water surface loses 12 Btu/hr for each degree of temperature difference between heated water and outside air. Formula: Area of spa in square feet x 12 x desired temperature rise = required heater output in Btu/hr.

Using the above equation and assumed temperature rise of 37F, you can size a heater for a 5x8' spa as follows: 40 sq. ft. x 12 = 480 x 37F desired temperature rise = 17,760 Btu.

The sizing determination is based on the number of Btu/hr necessary to *maintain* the desired spa water temperature. In the example, a heater with an output of 17,760 Btu must run almost continuously to do this. Generally, a heater with a 20,000 Btu output would be the minimum size required. But this size heater may take 4 or more hours to heat the water to the desired temperature. If you turn the heater off between soaks, you'll want a larger heater to heat water more quickly.

The heater-sizing guide on page 90 shows the time it takes for various-size heaters to heat different amounts of water.

HEATING COSTS

Heating costs for electricity and fossil fuels are calculated by units. Gas is priced per *therm*. One therm equals 100,000 Btu. Fuel oil is sold by the *gallon*. One gallon equals 140,000 Btu. Oil heaters typically consume

If heat is turned off between soaks, a properly sized gas heater can reheat the water in a matter of minutes.

fuel oil at a rate of 1 to 1.5 gallons per hour. Electricity is priced by the *kilowatt hour*. One kilowatt hour equals 3,412 Btu.

All Btu equivalents expressed here represent heater input—the total amount of heat generated by the fuel. The input-output ratio of a heater determines its heating efficiency, as discussed on the previous page. Use the heater's input rating when figuring heating costs.

Using the figures and information from the heater-sizing guide, you can compute heating costs as follows:

First, add the time required to heat the water initially to desired tempera-

If air blower and number of air holes in spa are matched correctly, water action should look like this.

To avoid back-pressure in the plumbing system, pump strainer basket should be cleaned at least once a month.

pressure for a standard installation with a 2-inch air line.

If a spa has a combination of different-size air holes, it's necessary to calculate how many of each size are needed to equal the 1.6-square-inch air line capacity. The following example shows this calculation:

Existing air holes:
25 1/8-inch holes and
20 5/32-inch holes

Multiply number of existing air holes by their surface area (from table):
25 x .0123 = .3075 sq. in.
20 x .0192 = .384 sq. in.

Add these figures to get the amount of air that can be released through air holes:
.3075 + .384 = .6915 sq. in.

Subtract this amount from the air-line capacity to see if there's back-pressure, and if so, how much:
1.6 − .6915 = .9085 sq. in.

If more air needs to be released, decide what size air holes will be drilled. Divide the decimal equivalent of the hole-surface area into the back-pressure amount to find the number of air holes needed.

For this example, using 1/8-inch air holes:
.9085 ÷ .0123 = 73.8 OR:
74 more 1/8-inch air holes must be drilled.

RECOMMENDATIONS
● When you need to angle pipe for the blower line, two 45° angles are preferable to one 90° angle.

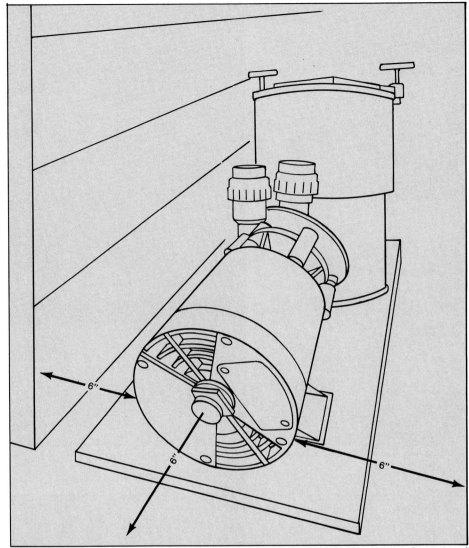

Allow adequate clearance between pump motor and surrounding decking, equipment and other surfaces. Keep ventilation openings in pump clean.

● If not enough air holes exist, more should be drilled, or better, existing holes made larger.

● In any system with more than 50 feet of air line, use 2-1/2-inch-diameter air line for the first 15 feet.

● Use a check valve in every system. It should be the flapper type rather than a spring check valve. If you use a loop in the air line, install it 12 inches above water level.

SUPPORT EQUIPMENT MAINTENANCE

The reliability and life expectancy of support equipment can be increased by proper maintenance. This seems obvious, but many spa and tub owners overlook it. A malfunctioning spa or hot tub is no fun. So take care of your equipment!

PUMP AND MOTOR MAINTENANCE

To keep from overheating, electric motors breathe in surrounding air. If that air contains moisture, dirt or chemicals, these elements will get into the system. Pump motors in particular must be well cared for. All wiring should be protected from water to prevent short circuiting.

To operate efficiently, electric motors require ample cross-ventilation. Ventilation openings in the motor should be kept clean. The motor should be placed at least 6 inches away from the spa or tub deck or other obstructions. Many pumps are set too close to the deck. As a result, water and dirt are sucked up into the motor.

Keep the area around the motor clean. Avoid sweeping or stirring dust

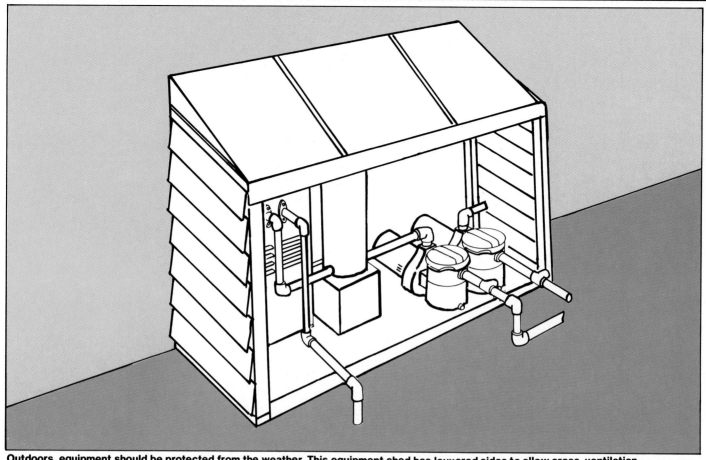

Outdoors, equipment should be protected from the weather. This equipment shed has louvered sides to allow cross-ventilation.

near the motor while it's running. Also avoid storing or spilling chemicals near it. If the motor is located in a spot where water collects, provide proper drainage. Repair leaky pipe joints or pump seals promptly.

If the pump is outdoors, cover it. This will protect the unit from the elements, especially sunlight and high humidity. High temperatures can be particularly damaging. Heat causes oil to separate out of grease in pump and motor bearings, which in turn allows bearings to run dry and fail.

A roofed shelter with horizontally-louvered sides will provide even more protection. Space the louvers to provide adequate ventilation to the motor. In addition, the shelter should clear the motor at all points by a minimum of 10 inches. If the heater will also be in the shed, follow manufacturers' instructions on correct clearances.

HEATER MAINTENANCE

Many spa and tub owners do not properly maintain their heaters. Failure to do so can lead to discomfort—cold water—and unnecessary expense.

Here are some tips to help you keep your heater in good working order.

Poor water chemistry will take its toll on the heat-exchanger's tubes and fittings. These components are usually made of copper. A chlorine tablet in the skimmer or pump basket dissolves, causing a high chlorine level in the water. When the pump is turned off, the chlorinated water sits in the heat exchanger eating away the metal parts. To prevent this, *do not* overchlorinate and *do not* put chlorine in the pump basket or skimmer. The same holds true for acid and other spa chemicals.

Other unwanted results can be produced by poor water chemistry. A thermostatically controlled bypass is built into the heater. Two or three years of bad water chemistry will cause *scale,* or chemical residue, to build up around this bypass. It will then become stuck. Complete instructions on proper chemical maintenance start on page 137.

Spa and tub owners often want the heater switch located near the house. This may mean an extra 300 feet of heater wire carrying a 700-millivolt

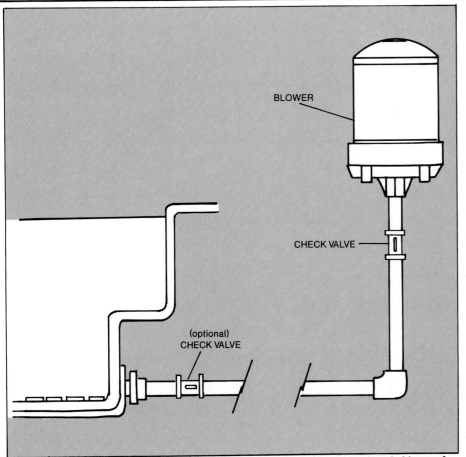

Install a check valve between air blower and spa to keep water from entering air-blower. A second valve can be installed near the spa to keep water out of the blower line.

current. The added wire resistance will reduce the pilot generator's life one to five years, or it may ruin the unit as soon as it's turned on. Check manufacturer's recommendations on the maximum amount of heater wire allowable for the unit you buy.

A gas-fired heater must be installed with its own separate fuel line. A line shouldn't be run from the supply of another appliance, such as a home water heater. The fuel line should be 1-inch-minimum-diameter pipe. Experts suggest using a larger pipe size in case you want to install a larger heater in the future.

Remember to "bleed" the gas line before starting up the heater. Bleed it until you begin to smell gas.

AIR-BLOWER MAINTENANCE

Air-blower failure is usually caused by motor burnout or melting of the plastic housing. Undersize pipes are often to blame. Dealers recommend PVC pipe with a minimum 2-inch diameter. This prevents back-pressure that causes blower failure.

It's also important to have the

proper size and number of air holes in your spa or tub bubbler ring. The volume of air going through the blower pipe has to get out. If it doesn't, it will overheat the motor.

Check to see if there are enough air holes in the spa bottom or bubbler ring. A standard recommendation for

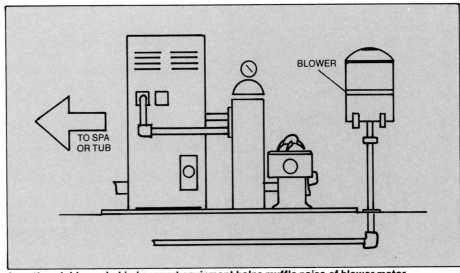

Locating air blower behind support equipment helps muffle noise of blower motor.

spas and tubs with 2-inch air lines is 58 3/16-inch holes. This size hole is especially important with fiberglass spas. Some spas come with holes smaller than this. Overhanging fibers block these smaller holes even though they may seem to be open.

Use a hand drill to clean fibers from the holes, but be careful. If you penetrate the second layer of fiberglass you may cause a leak. A small rattail file will also do the job. If the spa or tub comes with an insufficient number of air holes, refer to page 91 to determine how many more are needed. It's best to have a spa dealer or installer drill the holes.

Another common cause of blower failure is water damage. This problem can generally be solved through the use of a check valve. The check valve will prevent water backflow into the blower. It should be mounted vertically at least 24 inches above the water level of the spa or tub.

Use a check valve recommended by the air-blower manufacturer. It should seal when shut off and be able to hold up throughout the life of the unit. Make sure the check valve is designed for use on air blowers. Most installers use a flapper-type check valve for this purpose. If it's a spring-type, make sure the spring has less than 1/2-pound pressure at full open. More resistance also impairs performance and can cause damage to the air blower.

Some installers like to use two check valves. They put one at the air blower and one at the spa to keep water out of the spa-to-blower pipe. When the blower is turned on, air enters the spa much faster. The extra valve also adds an additional margin of safety. The location of the second valve is shown in the photo on page 119.

The same thing can be accomplished if a loop is plumbed into the air line. A loop is simply a series of right angles in the pipe that bring a short section of it above water level. It prevents water from running through the pipe from the spa or tub back to the blower.

Every precaution should be taken when installing air blowers. Never install an air blower below water level unless the manufacturer has approved such use. Correct installation will add years of trouble-free service and increase performance. For detailed information on installing air blowers, see page 127.

MOTOR NOISE

Another problem that has plagued air-blower manufacturers is motor noise. To generate sufficient air flow and pressure, these motors must run at 15,000 rpm to 22,000 rpm. Unfortunately, this makes them very loud. Air-blower manufacturers have worked hard to develop quiet, high-performance units.

New sound-proofing materials also help, but the units will never be *silent*. Judging from past warranty problems, installing motors underground to silence them doesn't seem to be the answer.

TROUBLE-SHOOTING

When there's a problem with the air system, the first thing to do is find out if the blower is working. If it isn't, check inside the blower nozzle for water damage. If the unit is water-damaged, it's because water has run back through the air line from the spa or tub. This means that the check valve on the air line has failed or a valve or loop wasn't installed to begin with. Replace or add a check valve when you repair or replace the damaged blower. Installing a loop in the air line will serve the same purpose as a check valve.

If the blower is running but not pumping air, or if it's noisy, excessive back-pressure may be the problem. More than 1 pound of back-pressure in the blower system will cause the motor to burn out. Turn it off immediately.

To correct a back-pressure problem, make sure the outlet holes are clean and the air line is free of obstructions. Check to see if you have the right-size line and the correct number of air holes. See page 91.

If the problem still exists, check the blower itself. First check the blower motor voltage against the line voltage. If a 220-V motor is hooked to a 110-V line, it will run at half speed. One of the pressure-chamber seals may have a hole or leak. Or the plastic enclosure may have warped, causing the air to recirculate. If replacement parts aren't readily available from your spa or tub dealer, send the unit back to the manufacturer for repair or servicing.

Do not use glue to connect the air

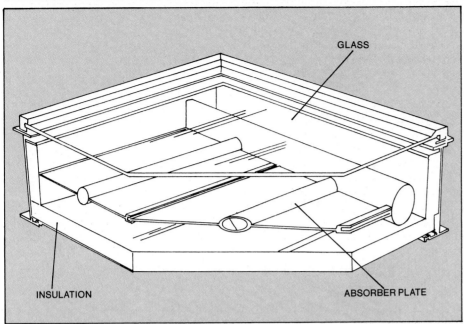

GLASS

INSULATION

ABSORBER PLATE

Glazed solar panel with tube-type absorber plates is considered most efficient for heating spas and tubs. Panels with stainless-steel tubes and pipes best resist corroding effects of chemically treated water.

blower to the inlet pipe. Fumes from glue may ignite when the motor is turned on. It also makes it difficult to remove the blower if it needs repair or replacement.

SOLAR HEATING

There's no doubt that solar heating for swimming pools is both practical and efficient. But the feasibility of solar heating for spas and hot tubs hasn't been proven.

At current utility rates, the installation of solar-heating equipment doesn't seem to be cost effective. This situation could change in the near future.

Why, then, use a solar-heating unit for your spa or hot tub? It will lower the amount of other energy, such as gas or electricity, that you use—in some cases dramatically. More than 30 states in the United States offer tax breaks on the cost of a solar system. There's the additional appeal of using an alternative, free source of energy. Some people fear that local restrictions will soon prohibit use of natural gas or electricity to heat spas and tubs.

If you want to use solar for a spa or tub only, most solar installers recommend using single- or double-glazed collector panels. Used for home hot-water systems, these panels provide the high temperatures necessary for spas and hot tubs.

If you have a swimming pool and spa, solar heating both units is practi-

cal and cost effective. The number of unglazed solar panels needed to heat the pool to 80F (27C) is sufficient to heat a spa to the 100F (38C) range.

Such installations often include programmable monitors. These devices route heat to the pool during the morning and early afternoon. They then divert heat to the spa at about 3 p.m. so it will be hot when the owners return home in the evening.

As solar technology becomes more sophisticated, the options in solar-heating systems increase. It would be impractical to try to describe all the systems available. The drawing on the next page shows how a basic solar-panel system works on a spa or hot tub.

WHERE TO START

The best place to begin shopping for a solar system is with a qualified solar engineer or consultant. Don't let the title scare you. In most cases, a solar engineer or consultant is employed by a firm that specializes in solar-heating installations.

You may need a professional to install the sytem. It's a good idea to bring such a person into the picture early to get as much information as possible.

There's no standardized name for solar consulting firms. Check the Yellow Pages under the headings, "Energy" and "Solar."

Ask about the range of services the

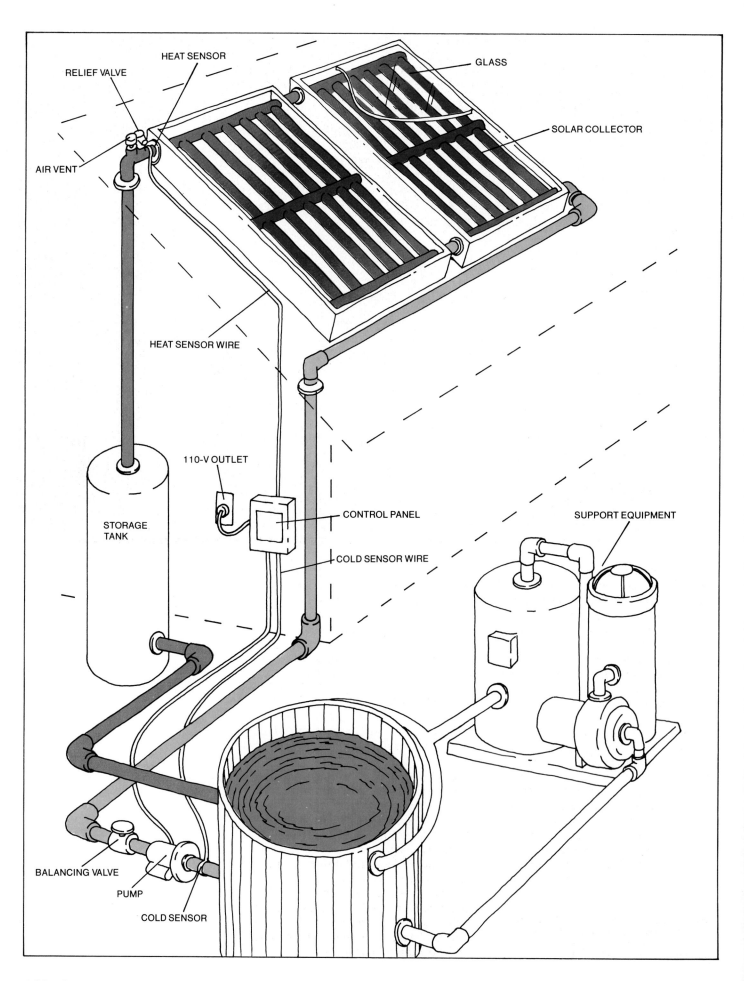

RELIEF VALVE

HEAT SENSOR

GLASS

SOLAR COLLECTOR

AIR VENT

HEAT SENSOR WIRE

110-V OUTLET

STORAGE TANK

CONTROL PANEL

COLD SENSOR WIRE

SUPPORT EQUIPMENT

BALANCING VALVE

PUMP

COLD SENSOR

Hot-tub cover helps prevent heat loss through the water's surface. Covering a spa or tub also keeps out leaves and other debris.

firm offers. Do they make the actual installation as well as consulting? What's the extent of their experience in solar systems? Ask for references of local customers. Be cautious with a company that endorses one specific line of components over another. Each situation has its own particular requirements.

The plastic-or-metal controversy continues as competition among manufacturers of solar collectors increases. Plastic collectors have been used to heat many pools and spas. But don't overlook the benefits of metal collectors—either copper, copper and aluminum, or stainless steel. Stainless steel best resists corrosion caused by chemically treated water.

The initial cost of a metal collector may be higher than plastic panels, but the life of a metal collector is longer.

Left: This drawing illustrates the basic principle of a solar heating system for a spa or hot tub. There are a number of variations on this basic design.

Metal collectors are structurally rigid. They're easier to secure to the roof than flexible plastic panels, so they're a better choice in windy areas.

No matter who you talk to about a solar system, get a drawing or plan showing how the plumbing will work. All solar systems should include freeze protection—a gravity drain that allows the water to flow out of the collector when the pump stops.

Make sure that the pump and pipes match solar collector requirements.

COMMON QUESTIONS ABOUT SOLAR HEATING

Following are frequently asked questions about solar-heated spas and hot tubs with answers that reflect the consensus of solar experts.

What's the first thing I must know about solar heating?

Solar heating can't do it all. The most sophisticated solar spas and hot tubs require a backup heater. The backup heater is used on cloudy days and extremely cold nights.

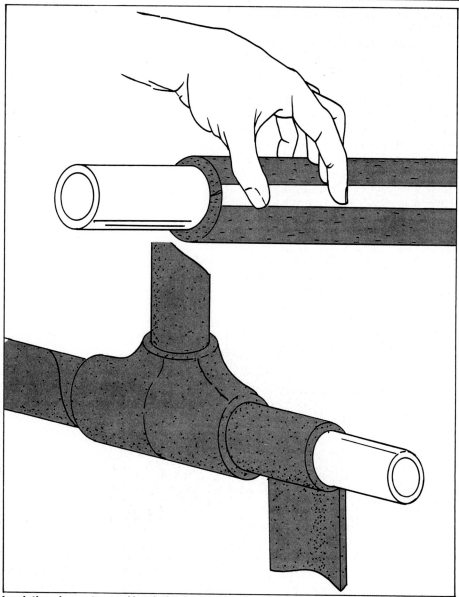

Insulating sleeve, top, and insulating tape help reduce heat loss through water pipes.

use the following formula: Find the number of Btu required to raise the water temperature in your spa or tub from tap level to 102F. To do that, multiply the number of gallons in the unit by 8.33 pounds, the water's weight per gallon. Then multiply the result by the number of degrees of temperature increase desired.

For example: 500 gal. x 8.33 lbs. per gal. = 4,165 lbs. Then 4,165 lbs. x desired temperature rise = number of Btu needed. If tap water temperature is 68F and desired water temperature is 102F, the desired temperature rise is 34F. So 4,165 x 34 = 141,610 Btu needed.

Next, multiply the number of hours in a solar day, six on average, by the number of Btu needed, as described above. Divide the answer by the number of Btu collected per panel per solar day. This will tell you the number of panels needed.

Where do you mount them?

Solar panels should face south. This is where you get the most sunlight. Panel angle in relationship to the sun depends on the latitude of your community. Solar installers in your area can tell you the proper angle.

Suppose my roof prohibits due-south position?

This isn't a serious problem. Solar panels can be mounted on a hill, garage, or in a back yard or garden —anywhere you can avoid shade.

Will solar collectors detract from the appearance of my property?

Not if they're located well and installed properly. If you mount the panels in the yard, a good landscape designer can offer advice on the best way to blend them into the surroundings.

HOW TO CONSERVE ENERGY

Water heat loss in spas and tubs is affected by *air temperature, humidity, wind speed* and *solar energy.* Controlling these factors conserves energy required to heat the water.

The best way to prevent heat loss is to insulate the spa or tub itself and insulate the plumbing system.

Insulating the body of water in the spa or tub will keep its temperature higher between uses. This means the heater doesn't have to work as hard to bring the water back up to the desired temperature.

Water in a spa or tub loses heat two

How much does solar equipment cost?

This depends on geographic region and type of solar collectors used. Within the United States, the equipment cost may run from $800 to $1,500 or more.

What's the payback on solar compared to gas and electricity?

You'll get many different answers to this question. Some dealers say it will take 30 to 40 years to recover the initial outlay for a solar system. Other authorities say the payback is much shorter. Payback could become irrelevant if solar heating becomes mandatory.

How many panels do I need?

First find out the heat output in Btu of the panels you'll be using. Then

ways—through the surface of the water and through the sides and bottom of the unit. Most of the heat loss is through the water surface.

The most effective way of preventing heat loss is by using a spa or tub cover. This offers the highest return on your initial investment in terms of reducing heating bills. Spa and tub covers are discussed in detail on page 52.

Spas and hot tubs also lose heat rapidly through their walls. This happens because they have relatively poor insulating properties.

Many fiberglass spas have foam insulation blown on the outside of the fiberglass shell. The thicker this coating is, the better. Laminated wood tubs with foam cores are also being tested.

Some manufacturers have developed insulating vinyl liners for hot tubs. These liners significantly reduce heat loss through exposed walls. The thickness and insulating qualities of the liner material determines the heat-loss reduction rate. Using both covers and liners is the most economical way to cut heating costs.

Insulating water pipes will reduce heat loss while water is circulating through the support system. One manufacturer says heat loss through pipes can be reduced nearly 50%. This means a monthly energy savings of 4 or 5 therms, or about $1.50 on a monthly gas bill. Savings with electric heaters is even greater. In cold climates, insulating water pipes is necessary to keep them from freezing.

Another way to save energy is to locate your spa or tub where it's protected from the wind. The less fluctuation in air temperature the spa or tub is exposed to, the less energy it will use. The drawing below shows how a wind screen protects a spa or tub.

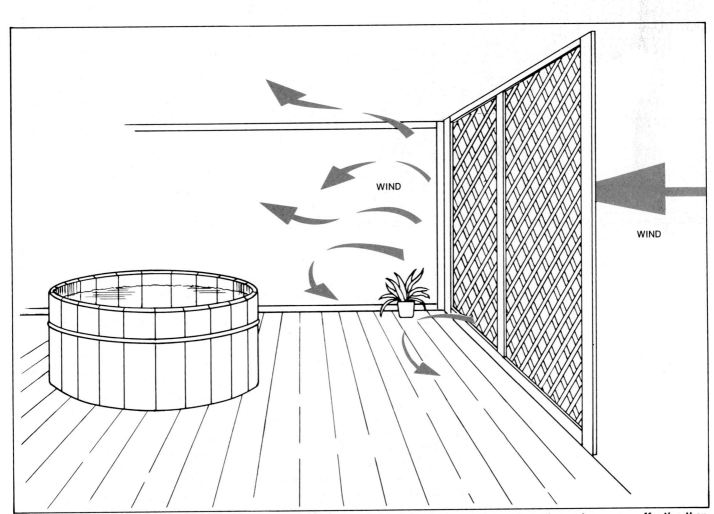

The cooling effect of wind can lower water temperature dramatically. Screens made of spaced slats or latticework are more effective than solid barriers in protecting the spa or tub from wind. Lattice screens provide the best protection when placed 6 to 12 feet away from the spa or tub.

Installing a Spa or Hot Tub

Installing a fiberglass spa or wooden hot tub is definitely something the average do-it-yourselfer can do. What's required is a basic knowledge of plumbing, a strong back, one or two helpers, and the ability to read diagrams and follow instructions precisely.

Most professional installers will tell you there are at least a dozen ways to install a spa or hot tub. Manufacturers' instructions vary. Each installation requires a slightly different approach. The object of this chapter is to offer general installation guidelines for fiberglass spas and wooden hot tubs.

They should be used in conjunction with instructions provided by the manufacturer of your spa or tub and its support equipment.

BEFORE YOU START

In the long run, careful planning may be the most important step in the installation. A little time spent planning saves a lot of time and trouble after work begins.

Two planning considerations are basic to the success of the installation. The first is the location of the spa or tub and its support equipment. This

Left: Worm's-eye view of fiberglass spa being set in excavation. You'll need several helpers for this job. Above: Support equipment is set on leveled precast concrete pads, arranged for easy hookup to plumbing lines.

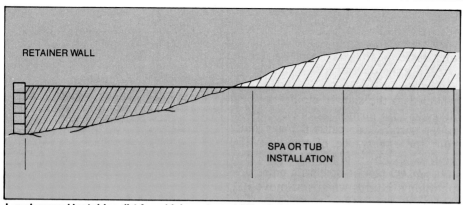

Level ground by taking dirt from high spots and filling in low ones.

Heavy building materials, such as bricks, lumber and sacks of concrete, should be stored as close to the site as possible. All lumber, including that for hot-tub kits, should be neatly stacked in an area that's not exposed to moisture or direct sunlight. These elements can warp wood if it's left outside more than a day or two.

PREPARING THE SITE

Once you have the site approved by the building department, the work of grading and excavation can begin. Clear the site of obstructions such as large rocks or unwanted plants. Consider removing nearby trees with extensive root systems because they can cause future problems with plumbing and masonry work.

Basic Installations—The drawings on the following pages show basic spa and tub installations. The type you've chosen, along with the site, determines the amount of grading and excavation needed. Also note the kinds of foundations used for each type.

GRADING

If the ground is flat, grading won't be necessary. If the site is on sloping or uneven ground, you'll probably need to level it, unless you're installing the unit on a hillside deck, as shown on page 43.

A general rule pertaining to spas states that you must have level ground around the spa equal to the depth the spa is sunk in the ground. For example, a spa set 3 feet in the ground requires 3 feet of level ground around its perimeter.

Some building departments now require that there be a minimum of 10 feet of level ground around a spa or hot tub, regardless of the depth of the installation. Check local codes.

Leveling the site is a simple process of cutting and filling, or taking dirt from the high spots and filling in the low ones. Stretching leveled string between stakes parallel to the slope of the site will help in leveling the ground beneath.

When grading the site, remember that the ground should slope slightly away from all sides of the spa or hot tub, once it's installed. This allows for water runoff, and is especially important for in-ground spas.

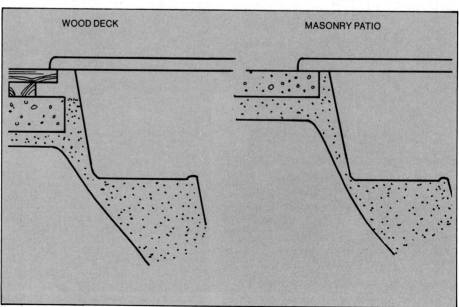

Plan excavation depth so lower edge of spa lip is flush with finished deck or patio.

EXCAVATION

Generally, there are two kinds of excavation required. The first is digging the hole for the unit itself. In-ground spas and tubs will require extensive excavation, though some digging may be necessary for the foundations of above-ground units.

The other is trenches for water, gas and electrical lines. Usually, you'll need one trench from the unit to its support equipment for water-circulation pipes. This trench may also contain lines for control switches. Another trench will carry the gas and electrical lines from the equipment to the main hookups at the house. Your plans may call for additional trenches if you want to install light fixtures or a water faucet near the installation.

Before you do any digging, recheck your plans to make sure you won't be running into any existing underground pipes or wires. Decide how you'll dispose of excess dirt from the excavation. Here are two other points to consider before excavating:

First, the rim of in-ground spas and tubs should be higher than the finished deck. This reduces the chance of dirt from washing into the water during rain storms or when hosing down the deck. Before excavating, determine the finished spa-rim height in relation to ground level.

Second, determine the position of the spa in the hole and where plumbing will go. If the spa or tub will have an underwater light, position the unit so the light points away from the house.

In-Ground Spas—The drawing above shows a typical in-ground spa excavation. Note how much space is left around the spa to allow for backfilling with sand. If you overdig or underdig the hole, you may have trouble seating the spa correctly. This can result in broken plumbing or a spa that isn't level.

With a shovel, dig the hole to the rough shape and contour of the spa. Overcut 4 inches to 6 inches on all horizontal surfaces and 10 inches to 15 inches on all vertical surfaces. This will allow space for plumbing and to backfill the excavation with sand once the spa is set in place.

The bottom of the hole should be firm, hard soil. It's the dirt underneath the spa, not the sand, that provides the stability your spa will require.

Determine where the plumbing

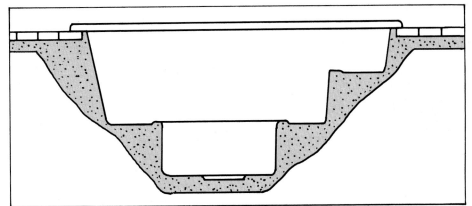

In-ground spas require no foundation. Spa is set in hole and backfilled with clean sand. Dig hole large enough to provide clearance for plumbing.

Excavation for spa and trenches for plumbing lines are all dug at once. Trench at left of photo leads from spa to support equipment. Trench in background leads to gas meter at back of property.

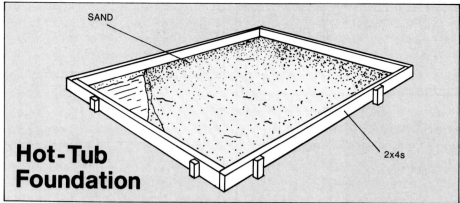

Hot-Tub Foundation

Build concrete form of 2x4s and 1x2 stakes as shown. Excavate 2 inches below bottom of forms and fill with clean sand.

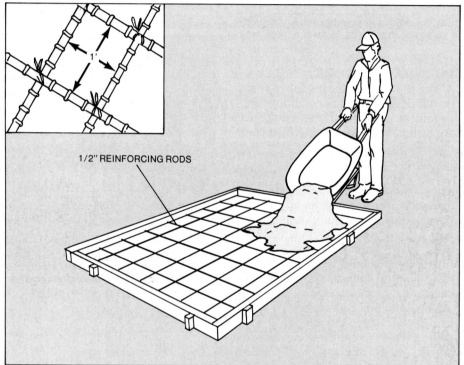

Lay a 1-foot-square grid of 1/2-inch reinforcing rods over leveled sand bed. Tie rods together with bailing wire. Mix concrete and pour it in the form. Spread concrete evenly with a sturdy steel rake.

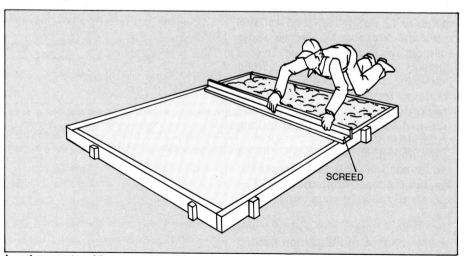

Level concrete with a screed built from 1x4s as shown. Pull the screed toward you with a side-to-side zigzag motion. When concrete is leveled, smooth out with a large mason's float. Allow concrete to cure at least two days before setting tub.

On solid, well-drained ground, pier blocks in concrete footings are sufficient support for a hot tub. Space piers 2 feet apart along chine joists.

shown in the drawing above. For this type of foundation, the pier blocks must be set in concrete footings and carefully leveled to the same height. Piers should be spaced about 2 feet apart under the chine joists.

The simplest and best foundation is a level, reinforced-concrete slab poured to match your particular tub. The drawing at left shows how to make this foundation. Generally, the pad should be 3-1/2 inches to 4 inches thick, and reinforced with steel rods on a 1-foot-square grid.

Do not set the tub on an existing concrete patio unless you're absolutely certain it will support the tub's weight. Most concrete patios are not reinforced, nor are they thick enough to support the weight of most tubs.

Foundations for below-ground tubs are somewhat more complex. In addition to a concrete floor, retainer walls are usually required to keep dirt from falling into the pit.

Support Equipment—The pump, filter and heater also require a level foundation. A 2-inch-thick pad of poured concrete or 2-inch patio blocks is adequate for most standard equipment. Some home-and-garden centers carry precast concrete pads in various sizes. Or you can make forms from 2x4s and pour your own pad.

The pad should be laid on a base of sand, several inches above ground level. This prevents water from settling around the equipment.

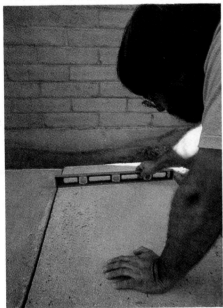

Precast concrete pads for support equipment must be perfectly level.

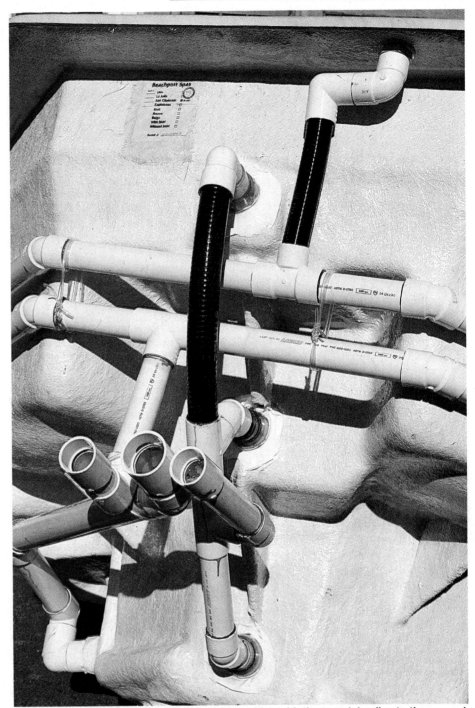

All pipes in preplumbed spa are stubbed out to align with the trench leading to the support equipment. Mark pipes to avoid making wrong connections after spa is set.

FIBERGLASS SPAS

Unless your spa is preplumbed, you'll have to install main and side drains, skimmer and hydrojet fittings. Once the fittings are installed, they're plumbed around the outside of the spa to the point where the trench will go.

You'll have to decide where you want to *stub out,* or end, the lines before you put the spa in the ground. Lines for jets, drain, skimmer and other fittings should be plumbed toward a common trench as shown in the photograph at right. All this must be done before the spa is set in place.

The drawings on pages 115-118 and 126-128 show plumbing diagrams for typical spa installations. Refer to them as you read to help identify the various components and how they're connected.

PREPLUMBING THE SPA

Check to make sure the spa has holes for the drain, skimmer and hydrojet fittings. If holes must be drilled, it's best to have a spa dealer or installer do the work. If you do the work yourself, check both sides of the spa before you drill, so you don't penetrate the air channel. Use the appropriate-size bit or hole-saw attachment. Drill from the inside spa surface to the outside.

Flexible PVC tubing is used to connect jets to individual air controls on spa lip.

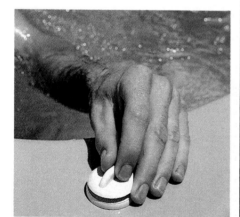

Individul air controls for each jet regulate air flow, increasing or decreasing hydrojet action.

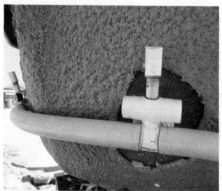

Short lengths of rigid PVC pipe are used to bypass horizontal air line connections. Pipes are then connected to air controls with flexible PVC tubing.

on the spa. The drain or drains will be plumbed to the circulating pump inlet.

There are several ways to plumb the air lines for the jets. On some installations, each jet has its own individual line that leads to an air-control valve. The valve is usually located on the spa lip above the water line, as shown in the photo at left. This setup allows you to adjust the action of each jet separately.

Jets can also be plumbed into a common air line, or manifold, which leads to a single air-control valve. The control valve can be located near the spa or the support equipment, or

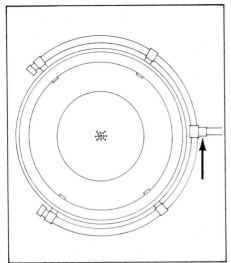

Tee the jet manifold to air and water supply lines midway between jets to equalize air and water flow.

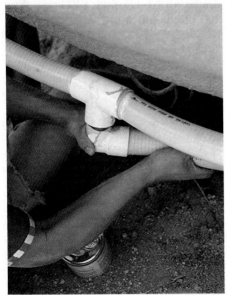

Plumb jet manifolds so they can be easily connected to the main supply lines.

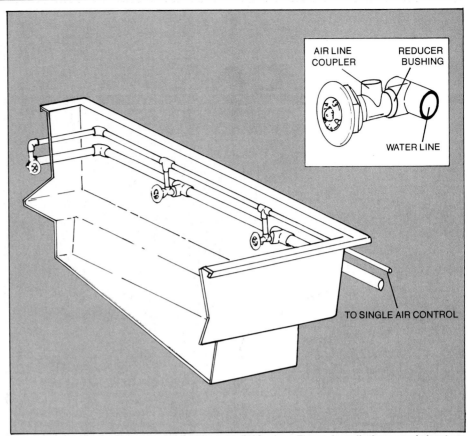

Tee jets are most often plumbed with rigid PVC pipe. These installations work best on square or rectangular spas.

whatever spot is convenient. The drawing above shows this type of installation.

When you push flexible pipe into the jet, *do not* turn the pipe *clockwise*. If you do, the pipe will expand and won't seat properly into the fitting.

To equalize water and air flow to the jets, it's not necessary to run air and water manifolds completely around the spa. Install tee fittings at the middle point of the air and water manifolds, as shown in the photos at left. If the spa has four jets, install the tee midway between the second and third jet.

Install the air and water manifold tees so they can easily be plumbed into the supply lines later. On most installations the tee openings face down. Flexible PVC is run from the tee to the support equipment.

If you're using tee jets, you'll need a 1-inch coupling to connect the jet wall fittings to the air manifold. To connect the jets to the water manifold, you may need a 1-1/4-inch to 1-1/2-inch *reducer bushing* to put over the water inlet side of the 1-inch coupling. First attach the coupling to the jet, then the bushing to the coupling, as shown in the drawing above.

Once the spa is preplumbed, gently set it in the excavation. You'll need at least two helpers. Be careful not to damage plumbing and fittings.

To level the spa, fill it with water to seat and gently rock spa back and forth. Check with a level frequently. Fill low spots under spa with sand.

Wet the sand until it flows into voids under the spa. This process is called *flowing* sand into the excavation.

SETTING THE SPA

While setting the spa, avoid scratching the spa's smooth interior surface. Keep the inside of the spa free of sand and dirt. Don't stand or walk inside the spa. Don't set tools in it.

Cover the bottom of the hole with a level layer of sand. For spas with bottom drain fittings, use 4 inches to 5 inches of sand. For spas with side drain fittings, use 2 inches to 3 inches of sand. If the spa has a bottom drain fitting, dig a small trench at the bottom of the hole to provide clearance for the drain plumbing.

Carefully lift the spa and set it in the excavation. You'll need at least two other persons to help. Do not lift the spa by its plumbing connections or fittings.

Check to make sure the top lip of the spa is at the proper level. If it isn't, you'll have to lift the spa out of the hole and either dig the hole deeper or put more sand in the hole.

With a carpenter's level and a 2x4, check level in all directions. Level the spa by rocking it gently.

Backfilling—When the spa is reasonably level, fill it with water up to seat. Backfill the excavation with wet sand up to the seat level. After putting several shovels of sand into the hole, use a garden hose to wet the sand. Use just enough water so the sand flows into the voids around the footwell area. If you use too much water the spa will float out of the hole.

While backfilling, check level frequently. Level the spa by flowing sand under the low points of the excavation.

Make sure sand is tightly packed

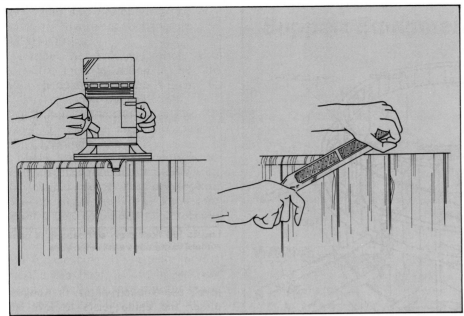

Use a Surform rasp or a router to round hot-tub edges.

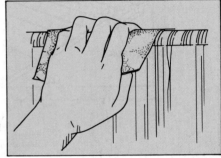

Sand edges smooth with a fine grit sandpaper.

under seats and around air channels. Be careful not to raise the spa above the desired height while backfilling. Do not get sand in the plumbing stubs at the head of the trench.

Once the spa area is backfilled to the seat level, set up the support equipment and connect it to the spa. See pages 125-129. When the spa is plumbed to the support equipment, an inspection will be required before final backfilling of spa excavation and trenches.

HOT TUBS

Installation procedures for installing hot tubs and spas are similar. The main difference is that a hot tub is not buried in the ground so no backfilling is required. Below-ground tubs require a pit with retainer walls, as described on page 110. The following instructions assume that all foundation work has already been done.

An above-ground tub can be plumbed before or after it's set on its foundation. But it must be plumbed before decking or surrounding masonry is installed. For a below-ground tub, it's easier to install pipes and fittings before the tub is lowered in the pit.

TUB FINISH DETAILS

If you're building your tub from a kit, the best instructions to follow are those that come with it. If you bought a preassembled tub, you may want to put some finishing touches on it before installation.

The square-cut stave tops can be sanded and shaped to a smooth, rounded finish if you wish. Use medium-grit sandpaper, a Surform tool, or a router with a 1/2-inch to 3/4-inch radius bit for the initial shaping. Use fine-grit sandpaper for the final finish.

Check the tub interior for any rough spots. Lightly sand these areas to eliminate any splinters. Sawdust from sanding can be left inside the tub. It helps seal the tub by filling small cracks until the wood swells.

SETTING THE TUB

Above-ground tubs can be set on the foundation before or after you install the jets and other fittings. It's sometimes easier to tip the tub on its side to install and plumb the floor drain. You may want to do this before the tub is set on the foundation.

It's better to plumb fittings to the head of the trench once the tub is set. That way, there's less chance of damaging the plumbing when the tub is moved.

For below-ground installations, do all preplumbing before the tub is lowered into the excavation. Determine at what point on the tub the plumbing will enter the trench. Plumb all pipes to this location.

Carefully lift the tub and set it on the foundation. Use a level and a 2x4 to check tub level. If the tub isn't

TIPS ON SOLDERING COPPER PIPE

If you're using copper pipe for plumbing the heater, you'll have to solder non-threaded connections. You'll need a propane torch and the appropriate solder and flux. These materials are sold at plumbing supply stores.

Soldering joints for copper pipe and connections is called *sweat soldering*. In this process, the heated pipe and connection, not the torch, is used to melt the solder.

Cut the pipe to the proper length and remove any burrs on the pipe end with a file. Test-fit the pipe in the fitting to make sure it slides in easily and seats properly. Clean the pipe end with steel wool, then coat it with soldering flux.

With the torch, heat both the pipe end and the fitting. When both are sufficiently heated, touch the solder to the joint. If the pipe and fitting are hot enough, the solder will start to melt.

Continue heating the fitting evenly, 1/2 inch to 1 inch behind the joint. As you apply the solder to the joint, it will be drawn toward the heated portion of the copper fitting. Run the solder around the joint, making sure not to melt the solder with the torch.

When you've finished soldering, quickly wipe excess molten solder from the joint before it cools.

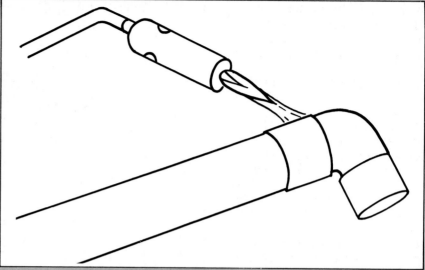

1. Heat pipe and fitting to a temperature that will melt the solder when touched to the joint.

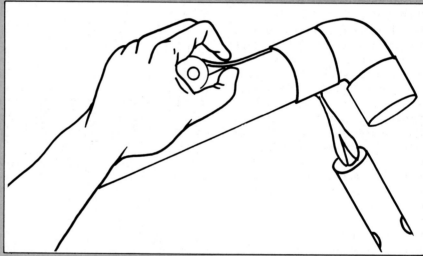

2. Feed solder into joint while applying heat to fitting behind.

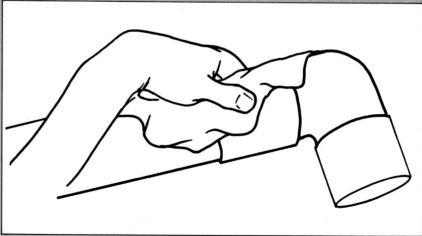

3 Wipe excess solder from joint with a clean, heavy rag.

hydrojet manifold tee or the hot-water inlet on the unit, or it may go to both locations.

MOUNTING THE EQUIPMENT

If you haven't already chosen a location for your support equipment, see page 104. You'll need a foundation for the equipment, as described on page 112. You'll also need trenches from the equipment to the spa or tub and to electrical and gas hookups at the house. Do this work before installing the equipment.

Preplumbed skid packs should be mounted on the foundation according to manufacturer's instructions. If you're installing components individually, you may have to assemble them before they're mounted on the foundation.

Gas heaters may need certain adjustments before being installed. At high elevations, the heater will have to be properly calibrated to compensate for altitude. A local dealer will be able to help you.

If the heater is using propane, make sure it has the proper jet fittings. If the spa or tub is located 3 or more feet above the level of the heater, check with your dealer about calibration of the pressure switch.

Arrange the pump, heater and filter on the foundation so they can be plumbed together easily. Align the equipment as close as possible to trenches for plumbing and utility hookups. Follow manufacturer's instructions for mounting the equipment on the foundation pad.

When mounting the equipment, make sure you know where the inlets and outlets are located for each component.

To minimize noise, you can locate the air blower behind the other support equipment. To do this, run a trench for the blower pipe underneath the equipment foundation.

EQUIPMENT PLUMBING

All support equipment except a gas heater can be plumbed with flexible or rigid PVC pipe. See page 133 for instructions on plumbing with PVC pipe. You'll need to run metal pipe a specified distance from heater inlets and outlets. This is done to dissipate heat. Check manufacturer's instructions and local code requirements.

The drawings on page 78 show two typical support-equipment setups.

In tight quarters, flexible PVC can be used for all lines from support equipment to spa or tub. Note PVC-to-metal adapters on heater lines.

The sequence in which you plumb the support equipment depends on your particular installation. The following sequence is used for plumbing one-pump systems and circulating pumps for two-pump systems. On a two-pump system, the booster pump for the hydrojets is plumbed directly to the jet manifold, bypassing the circulating pump, filter and heater.

Connect the circulating pump to the filter, following the directions supplied with each unit. Cut pipe to proper length and connect to the pump outlet. If the outlet has an

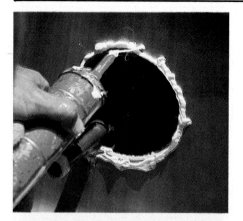

Underwater lights should be installed by a qualified electrician. Liberal use of silicone seal on both sides of spa wall is the secret to a leakproof installation.

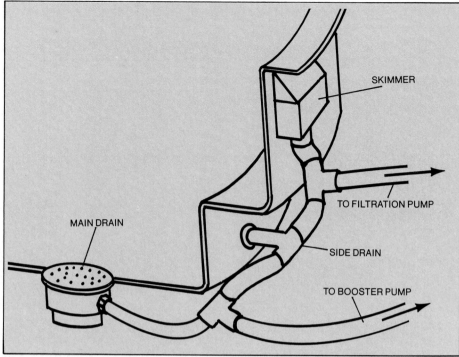

Use a tee fitting to connect jet booster pump inlet to main drain line, as shown.

from the heater to the appropriate hot-water inlet or inlets on the spa or tub. On one-pump systems, the return line is connected to the hydrojet manifold tee.

On two-pump systems, the line is connected to the hot-water inlet fitting on the spa or tub. On some one-pump systems, the line is plumbed to both the jets and the hot-water inlet. Gate valves are installed to direct the hot-water to the desired location. See drawing on page 127.

You must use metal pipe for the first 3 feet to 4 feet of the hot-water return line from the heater outlet, depending on local code requirements. Connect the copper pipe to PVC pipe with the appropriate PVC-to-metal adapter. See information on connecting filter to heater, beginning on page 126.

Connect the suction line between the circulating pump and the drain-skimmer outlet on the spa or tub. If the pump is below water level, a gate valve or ball valve should be installed in the line near the pump so water isn't lost when the filter is being changed.

If you have a two-pump system, run lines between the spa or tub and the booster pump for the hydrojets. Screw PVC adapters into the hydrojet booster-pump inlet and outlet. Remove the strainer basket when plumbing the pump.

The suction line to the booster pump inlet is connected to the drain plumbing. A tee fitting is generally used for this connection, as shown in the drawing above. The return line from the pump outlet is connected to the tee fitting on the hydrojet manifold.

Connect the line from the air blower to the spa air-channel outlet or bubbler-ring outlet on the hot tub. Unless the air blower is located 12 inches or more above the water line of the spa or tub, plumb a loop in the line as shown in the drawing on page 127.

If the blower line is more than 20 feet long, install a second loop as close as possible above the lip of the spa before it is run back to the equipment. See page 118 for details.

When making connections, *do not* use PVC glue for the final connection from the line to the blower outlet. Make the connection with a hose clamp. PVC glue is highly flammable, and the fumes could ignite when the blower is turned on. For the same reason, do not run the blower for 24 hours after making connections.

If the spa or tub has an underwater light, have a qualified electrician install it. Most codes require that the junction box for the light cord be at least 12 inches above the water level of the spa or tub. The circuit requires a GFCI breaker.

Time clock, switchbox and electrical subpanel are mounted on wall near support equipment for easy wiring. They should be located for easy access.

When you're finished making connections between the spa or tub and support equipment, make sure all joints are glued and the lines are hooked up correctly. Once you have double-checked your connections, you should be ready to run a pressure-test.

Though pressure-testing the lines isn't required by all building departments, it's a good idea to do it. Even if you've done the installation up to this point, it's best to have a spa or tub installer make the pressure test. He has the proper equipment to do the job.

UTLILITY HOOKUPS

Once the spa or tub is connected to the support equipment, electrical lines are run from the equipment to the main service panel at the house. The gas heater line is usually run in the same trench, then branched off to the gas meter.

At this point, it is recommended that you hire a licensed electrician to do all electrical wiring and hookups. Even if you are confident in your ability to wire the support equipment and run lines to the service panel, you should have a licensed electrician doublecheck your work and make the final connection at the panel. Many professional spa and tub installers do the same.

It's still a good idea to become familiar with the electrical requirements

of the installation. Then you can be assured that work is being done properly.

Electrical Requirements—Separate circuits are required for each piece of equipment. Check the main-service panel at the house to see if it has room for additional circuit breakers. If it doesn't you'll have to rewire the panel or have a subpanel installed.

Support equipment requiring electrical lines includes pump, blower, electric heater and underwater light. You can run additional lines for outdoor lighting or other electrical accessories in the same trench.

There are a number of code requirements and precautions regarding electrical wiring for spas and tubs. Check the local building department to find out what they are. Most codes require the following:

• All electrical equipment must be bonded, or grounded, to a hose bib, metal plumbing pipe or a grounding rod driven in the ground near the spa equipment. All support equipment, including some gas heaters, have a grounding lug for attaching the bond wire. Use No. 8 bond wire for bonding equipment.

• Normally, all metal parts within a code-specified distance from the spa or tub must also be bonded. This includes handrails, metal posts, metal door frames and metal window frames that may be nearby. Check codes for required distances.

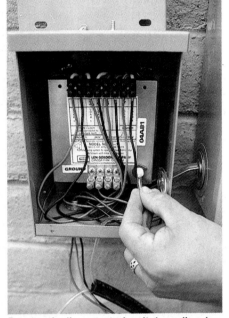

Pneumatically operated switches allow hydrojets, air bubbler and underwater light to be operated from spa. Switchbox is connected to spa-side controls by a small plastic tube, as shown. Short bursts of air through tube operate switches. All wiring is located a safe distance away from water.

pressure-test. The test must be checked by the building inspector. Call him for your rough gas inspection at this time.

To run the test, you'll need a pressure tester and gage. These are available at plumbing suppliers and spa dealers. Gas lines must hold a pressure required by local codes. Check with the building department before running the test.

Once the pressure test has been made, reconnect the line to the gas meter and heater. You can now turn on the gas and relight all the appliance pilots in the house.

Do not light the heater until you've filled the spa with water and made your final equipment tests.

COMPLETING THE INSTALLATION

At this point, the installation should have passed the electrical, gas and pressure-test inspection. All plumbing between the spa and equipment should be completed and the spa should be in the ground at the proper level.

Remove test plugs from the jets, drains and the skimmer. Uncap the hydrojet air line, if necessary.

Clean the spa or tub before your final test. Remove all sand and dirt from the inside surface. Gelcoat spas should be polished before being filled with water. See page 143.

Fill the spa or tub with water to a point just above the skimmer level. Make sure all the pipes have water in them. If you notice some leakage between the staves of your wooden tub, do not be overly concerned. The leakage should stop when the wood swells.

Testing The Equipment—The spa excavation should be backfilled to seat level at this point. Following manufacturer's instructions, turn on the equipment. If you have a gas heater, let the system run a few minutes before lighting it.

When lighting a gas heater, make sure the gas is turned on at the meter. Loosen the union at the heater to allow the gas to fill the entire line and bleed the excess air and glue fumes from the pipe. Bleeding the line through the pilot takes considerably longer.

Before starting the pump, make sure it is primed with water. Check to see that the strainer basket has water in it. When the motor is on, the pump

should prime within one or two minutes. If you run the pump dry, you can damage it and void the pump warranty.

Check all the equipment to make sure everything is running properly. If you have any doubts, immediately shut down the equipment and call your dealer.

With the equipment running, make a final check on the plumbing connections. If there are no leaks, you can backfill the trenches and other excavations.

Spas—For a spa, finish backfilling with clean sand, flowing it into the excavation with water from a garden hose. While backfilling, check to make sure the spa remains level and at the proper height. Be careful not to get any sand inside the spa. To avoid this, tape plastic sheeting over the top of the spa while backfilling. Make sure the sand is firmly packed around the spa, so there are no voids. Be careful not to damage plumbing while shoveling sand into the excavation.

Once the installation is complete and the excavation is backfilled, do any final grading. The ground around the spa or tub should have a slight slope away from the unit for a distance of about 10 feet. Use a shovel and steel rake to level and smooth the ground around the spa or tub.

Install drain covers and replace hydrojet eye sockets. Put the leaf basket inside the skimmer and install the weir gate.

Trim the skimmer opening with a razor blade or a sharp knife. For fiberglass spas, use a rasp to trim excess figerglass around the skimmer opening, if necessary. Make sure the weir gate moves back and forth freely.

Finishing Touches—You are now ready to test and chemically balance the water, as described in the next chapter. Once the water is balanced, you can use the spa or hot tub. At this point, you may want to complete any surrounding decking or masonry work before you take your first soak.

Finally, when your spa or tub is clean, hot and ready to go, check the temperature with a thermometer. It may take a little experimenting to find the temperature just right for you. Now, your work is finished and the enjoyment begins. A little simple maintenance will keep your spa in good working order and give you years of pleasure. Enjoy.

Trim skimmer opening in spa wall flush with skimmer faceplate. Make sure weir gate operates freely.

PLUMBING WITH PVC PIPE

Most plumbing for spas and tubs is done with PVC, or *polyvinyl chloride,* pipe and fittings. There are two basic kinds of PVC pipe: flexible and rigid. Flexible PVC pipe is most often used to preplumb drain, jet and other fittings on the spa or tub. Both rigid and flexible PVC pipe can be used in the trench from the spa or tub to the support equipment. Rigid PVC is slightly more difficult to use, but is about half as expensive as flexible PVC, and more readily available. When using flexible PVC, trenches do not have to be perfectly straight.

Flexible and rigid PVC pipe require different types of glue. A plumbing dealer can tell you which type of glue to use for each.

The diameter and wall thickness of the pipes are determined by local building codes. You'll need a special PVC pipe for running gas lines. It's marked *natural gas* right on the pipe. Install the pipes so the building inspector can see the markings during inspection.

PVC pipe connections are easy to do, but they must be done correctly or they'll leak. PVC pipe comes threaded and unthreaded. PVC glue and a special primer are used to connect unthreaded pipe to fittings. The primer is applied to both parts before gluing. Silicone seal is used with threaded PVC pipe and fittings.

Here are some general tips for working with PVC:
● Trial fit all pipes and fittings before gluing them together.
● Use a hacksaw or handsaw with a fine-tooth blade to cut pipe. Remove burrs from cut end with sandpaper, a file or a sharp knife.
● After coating with primer, apply a light coat of glue to the fitting, a heavy coat to the pipe. Be generous with glue, but don't apply too much or it will block the pipe opening.
● PVC glue dries quickly. Con-

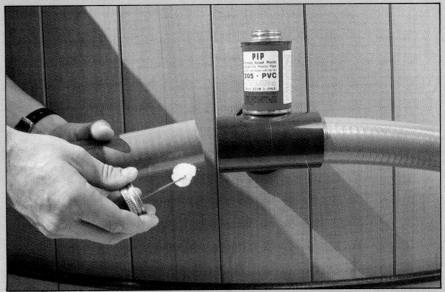

Flexible PVC pipe requires a special glue. Another glue is used for connecting PVC pipe to ABS plastic fittings.

PVC glue dries fast, so work quickly!

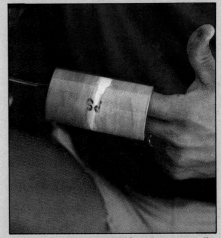

Before gluing, use PVC primer on all connections. Coat pipe with primer an inch or so beyond connection so the building inspecter can see it.

nect *immediately* after gluing. Glue should still be wet when the connection is made.
● When connecting unthreaded pipes to fittings, twist pipe one-quarter turn to spread glue evenly around connection, then align pipe and fitting. Hold connection together for about 1 minute until glue dries.
● When gluing flexible PVC pipe, use medium-grit sandpaper to roughen pipe ends before applying the glue. This will improve the bond when you glue the pipe to the fitting. With flexible-pipe glue, you'll have to

hold the joint together about 3 minutes to 10 minutes.
● If you make a mistake and have to disconnect flexible PVC from the fitting, don't remove the pipe from a glued joint. Cut the pipe 6 inches to 12 inches from the joint. Make the necessary adjustments or repairs, then join the flexpipe ends with a coupler. You can get couplers at plumbing suppliers.
● When connecting threaded PVC fittings, apply a generous coat of silicone seal to the male connection, which is the pipe with outside threads.

WINTERIZING YOUR SPA OR TUB

In cold climates, dealers offer winterizing kits like this one.

If you live in a climate where temperatures stay below freezing most of the winter, you must protect an outdoor spa or tub, equipment and plumbing.

Spa dealers in cold areas may offer freeze-protection packages that generally include:

● Insulation for the spa or tub itself.

● Insulation for pipes and support equipment.

● An insulated spa or tub cover to retain heat in the unit.

● One of several types of freeze-protection devices operated either by a time clock or a thermostat.

Dealers can also recommend other ways to prevent cold weather from damaging the spa or tub and its equipment.

Insulation—First, insulate the spa or tub itself. You'll need to insulate the side walls and use an insulated cover to retain heat in the main body of water.

Before installation, spas should be insulated with 1 inch to 2 inches of polyurethane foam before they're installed. Or partially backfill the excavation with styrofoam pellets—the kind used for packing material. A tub can be insulated in a similar manner below the decking surface. Fiberglass batts or blankets can be used on parts of the tub that are not visible.

Next, provide protection for the pipes. This is done after the plumbing is connected and before backfilling the trenches. Insulating pipe tape and pipe sleeves are available at most plumbing supply stores. You can also insulate the air line for the hydrojets with a special heat

tape, which is similar in principle to an electric blanket. It's the same type used in cold climates to keep car batteries from freezing. You'll have to provide a 110-V outlet. Check local codes to see if heat tape is approved for this use.

The best way to protect support equipment is to put it in an insulated enlosure. If possible, the enclosure should be in or attached to the house so it can be heated.

To keep water from freezing, it should be heated and circulated periodically. Freeze-protection devices are programmed to do this. These consist of a thermostat that reads either water or air temperature and is programmed to turn on the heater and pump when the temperature drops below a certain level. The water-temperature sensor should be located in the plumbing where the coldest water collects. This is usually in the suction line near the main drain.

Another type of freeze-protection device is operated by a time clock that turns on the pump at regular intervals. All of these devices must be set so they will protect the system without running too frequently and wasting energy.

If you want to shut down the spa or tub during the cold season, seek advice from a qualified dealer or installer in your area. Also read the instructions that come with the spa or tub and its support equipment. Some dealers will shut down the system for a small fee.

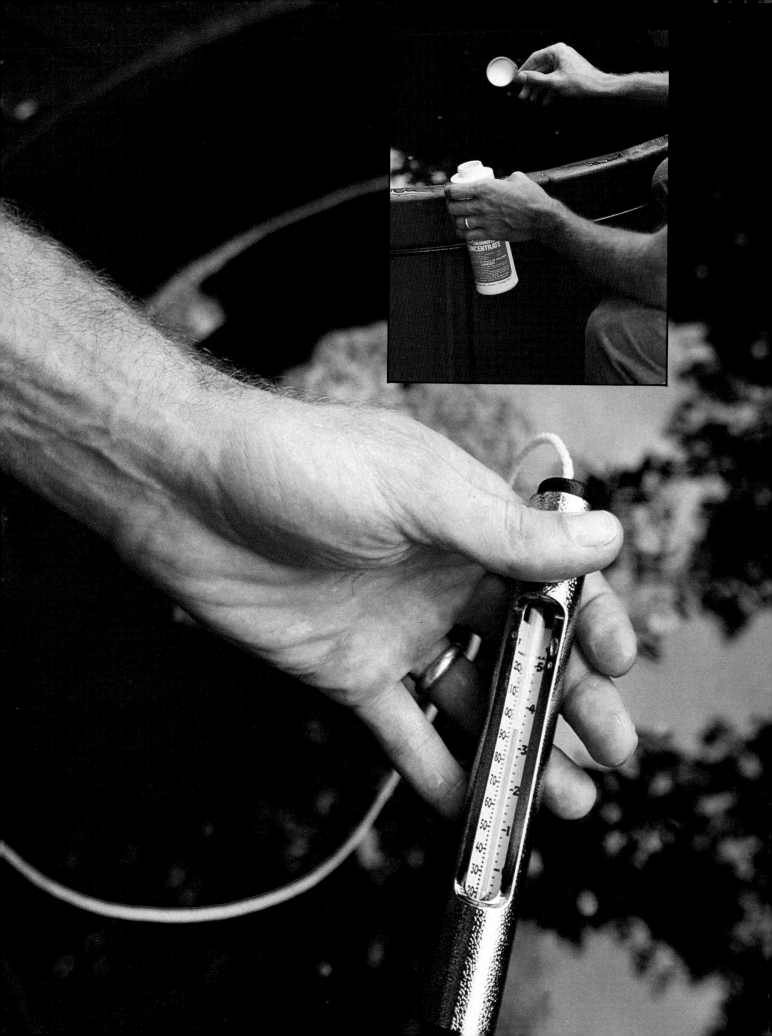

The biggest threat to a spa or hot tub is poor basic maintenance. Chemical maintenance of hot water is neither difficult nor complex. But it's *important* and it *must* be done on a regular basis.

Why is maintenance so important? According to an article in *Spa & Sauna Trade Journal:*

"The water volume of an average spa or hot tub seems modest when compared to a medium-size swimming pool. But when you add three bodies to the tub, it's equivalent to a crowd of over 200 people in a 20x40-foot pool. Then heat the water to 100F (38C) to provide ideal growth conditions for bacteria and algae. The disinfectants that don't evaporate quickly can be blown away by the bubblers and jets. Now all you have to do is neglect the necessary maintenance procedures. Soon you'll have a life-size petri dish of viruses, bacteria, algae and gunk.''

It doesn't have to be this way—you just have to understand chemical maintenance and stick to a regular program.

Spas and tubs are as easy, maybe easier, to maintain than a swimming pool. But there's a big difference.

Left: Adding the proper chemicals on a regular basis will keep spa and tub water sparkling clean. A spa or tub thermometer is useful to check temperatures before adding chemicals and using the unit. Above: Many spa and hot-tub dealers carry a complete line of maintenance products.

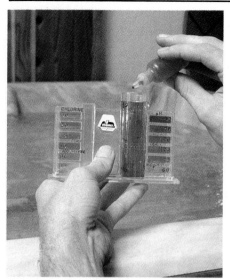

A good-quality test kit will tell you when water needs to be balanced and sanitized. Some even indicate the amount of each chemical necessary to treat the water.

It's enough to test pools once or twice a week and add chemicals once a month. But a spa or tub should be checked *every day*. You won't have to add chemicals each time, but you must test the water regularly because it can change rapidly.

What do you need to keep your spa or tub sparkling and germ-free? You must have a complete, good-quality test kit. The kit should contain equipment for testing disinfectant level, pH, total alkalinity and calcium hardness.

And you must understand what certain chemicals are used for and how they work. Too often, spa and tub owners have inadequate knowledge of what they're trying to accomplish with chemicals. There are two basic goals in hot-water maintenance: Sanitizing and balancing the water.

SANITIZING WATER

Keeping spa or tub water *sanitary* means keeping it free of living mi-croorganisms, including harmful bacteria. It also means preventing algae from growing in it.

Chlorine—This water disinfectant comes in three forms. Only one of the forms, *sodium dichlor,* is recommended for use in spas and hot tubs.

When added to the water, chlorine immediately attacks and kills living microorganisms and organic matter such as algae. In the process, a portion of the chlorine is used up or neutralized. The amount neutralized at any one time is called the *chlorine demand.*

The leftover chlorine—that which isn't neutralized—is known as *free chlorine.* Free chlorine is free to work as soon as it's needed. This is what a test kit measures.

Chlorine effectiveness is hampered by the presence of ammonia and other forms of nitrogen in water. Sunlight, water temperature and amount of spa or tub use also influence chlorine effectiveness.

Chlorine is available in three forms:

In addition to regular water-maintenance chemicals, special clarifiers can be used to keep water crystal clear. Clarifiers are not essential to spa or tub maintenance, but they do help make spas like this one look their best.

gas, liquid and *dry.* Using chlorine in gas form is complicated and is usually done only in large swimming pools.

Liquid chlorine, s*odium hypochlorite,* is widely used in home swimming pools. The actual chlorine content of liquid chlorine is 1-1/2 pounds chlorine salt per gallon. That small amount rapidly dissipates in the high temperatures of spa and tub water.

In addition to dissipating rapidly, liquid chlorine raises the pH level of the water. For a definition of pH level, see below. This must be countered with acid, or by partially replacing the water.

Dry, granulated chlorine is the favored form for spas and hot tubs. There are several types of granulated chlorine available—make sure you get the right one.

The types of dry chlorine you'll most often see are *calcium hypochloride, sodium dichlor* and *sodium trichlor.* Calcium hypochloride consists of chlorine and calcium in powder or tablet form. Because of the calcium content of calcium hypochloride, scale deposits on the spa or tub and its support equipment become a problem. A chemical stabilizer is required to maintain water balance.

Sodium dichlor is a neutral powder with a pH of 6.5 to 7.0. It's usually sold in a quick-dissolving granular form. The chlorine content of sodium dichlor averages a little less than 60%. It's an effective germicide and algaecide, and is considered the best type of chlorine for spas and hot tubs.

Sodium trichlor is generally sold in tablet, stick or cartridge form. It's usually used in conjunction with a dispenser. The chlorine content of sodium trichlor is 90%, making it hard to add the proper amount to a spa or tub. In addition, sodium trichlor has a very acidic pH of 2.6 to 3.0.

Bromine—Another chemical that's often used for sanitizing spa and tub water is *bromine.* It sanitizes water the same way as chlorine, but has several advantages. Bromine doesn't evaporate from the water as quickly as chlorine. This makes it especially suitable for the high water temperatures of spas and tubs. Also, bromine doesn't have the strong odor that chlorine does. Finally, it doesn't cause the eye irritation associated with chlorine.

There are two major bromine-based spa and tub sanitizers on the market.

One is a bromine-chlorine solution. Another is a two-chemical treatment.

In the two-chemical system, the water is initially treated with a sodium-bromide solution. This remains inert until an oxidizing agent is added, which releases a portion of the sodium bromide in the form of bromine. Daily treatments with the oxidizing agent are continued until the sodium bromide solution is used up.

Follow manufacturer's instructions when using these products.

There are other methods of sanitizing water. Non-chemical water purification systems are available for use as backup systems for chlorine sanitation. These systems are described on page 80.

BALANCING WATER

Balancing water means establishing proper balance among pH, calcium hardness, total alkalinity and total dissolved solids. Unbalanced water can corrode the spa or tub or leave mineral deposits. It's also hard on the support equipment. Remember that each factor in maintaining water balance is related to the others. Each must be at the proper level for the water to be balanced.

pH LEVEL MAINTENANCE

The *pH, potential hydrogen,* is the measurement of the relative acidity or alkalinity of any solution. The pH scale runs from 0, which is extremely acid, to 14, extremely alkaline. The middle of the scale, 7, is the neutral point. The ideal pH range for spa and hot-tub water is 7.2 to 7.8, depending on the average water temperature. See page 142.

Too high a pH promotes scaling, clouding, carbonate residue, eye irritation and difficulty in maintaining proper chlorine levels. Too low a pH makes spa or tub water corrosive. It may etch plaster and copper pipes, stain spa walls and cause rapid loss of chlorine.

Adjusting and maintaining proper pH levels in spas and hot tubs can sometimes be difficult. This is especially true if pH balance has been allowed to reach too high or low a level.

The pH should be constantly maintained in the proper range. If a daily test indicates a low pH, raise it by adding soda ash—sodium carbonate.

Chemicals for spa and tub maintenance come in concentrated and ready-to-use forms. Follow manufacturers' instructions for use.

If the test indicates a high pH, lower it by adding acid—sodium bisulfate—or by replacing some of the water with fresh water. The chart on page 149 gives the correct pH levels for spas and tubs at various water temperatures.

Size difference makes it difficult to treat a spa or tub with the same instructions given for swimming pools. It's easy to recommend addition of 2 pounds of soda ash to a 20,000-gallon outdoor pool. But how do you treat a 450-gallon spa?

A simple method for resolving measurement problems is to create a dilute solution of the needed chemical. It will be less harsh than the concentrated chemical and safer to use. It's also much easier to add proper amounts using common measuring utensils. This is especially true with acid. Undiluted acid is hard on spa and tub surfaces and support equipment. *Never* use undiluted acid in a spa or hot tub.

To make the dilute solution, you'll need:

- A clean, 1-gallon, heavy-walled plastic jug for each chemical used. Jug should have a secure-fitting screw top.
- Clear-plastic measuring cups: 1-cup, 1/2-cup and 1/4-cup measures.
- A plastic tablespoon.
- A plastic funnel for pouring chemicals into jugs.

Measure all quantities *exactly*. Read manufacturers' label instructions and precautions. Clearly mark chemical name on all jugs.

To Lower The pH—To the 1-gallon plastic jug, add 2 quarts of room-temperature water. Carefully add 2 level cups of dry acid, sodium bisulfate. Mix the solution until all material has dissolved. Finally, dilute mixture to the 1-gallon level by filling the jug to the neck with room-temperature water. *When diluting any kind of acid, always put the water in first, then add the acid. Never pour water into a concentrated acid solution.*

To Raise The pH—Add 2 quarts of room-temperature water to the plastic jug. Carefully add 2 level cups of soda ash, sodium carbonate. Tighten cap securely and mix solution until all material has dissolved. Finally, dilute mixture to the 1-gallon level by filling jug to the neck with room-temperature water.

After testing the water's pH level, add the proper amount of the required solution from the tables on page 147 directly to the spa water. Pour slowly around the perimeter of the spa or tub. *Never* pour the solution directly into the skimmer. Whenever you add either solution, keep the circulation system of your spa or tub *on* to ensure good mixing.

After adding a dilute solution, continue to circulate the water for at least one hour. Then retest to make sure the pH is at the proper level. If the test shows the pH is still above or below the desired range, repeat the procedure.

CALCIUM HARDNESS

Calcium is one of the minerals that contributes to hard water. As far as water balance is concerned, it's the most important one to watch. The amount of calcium in water is measured in parts per million, or ppm. The ideal level is 150 to 300 ppm.

Contrary to what was once thought, some calcium is necessary in water for it to be balanced and prevent corrosion. Too little calcium hardness, or CH, makes water corrosive. Too much calcium hardness can throw water out of balance.

Altering Calcium Hardness—To lower CH use a *sequestering agent*,

1-GALLON PLASTIC JUGS

PLASTIC FUNNEL

PLASTIC MEASURING CUPS AND SPOON

If you buy chemicals in concentrate form, you'll need these items for making dilute solutions and adding them to the water.

available at spa and pool dealers. Follow manufacturer's directions for use.

To raise CH, use a dilute solution of *calcium chloride* in these proportions: 1 pound of chemical to 1 gallon room-temperature water. The table on page 146 shows recommended doses of dilute solution to increase CH.

Turn on the circulatory system of the spa or hot tub. Pour the prescribed dosage of dilute solution directly into the water. Continue circulating for 1 hour to ensure good mixing. Then check the pH of the water. Slight changes in pH may occur. Adjust if necessary.

It's best to reduce CH by draining and adding new water, provided the water to be added has a lower CH. If the water in your area is exceptionally hard, such as over 500 ppm, special adjustments to pH and total alkalinity will be required.

TOTAL ALKALINITY

Total alkalinity is the combined measurement of a group of alkaline salts in water. The alkaline family contains some members that are beneficial and some that cause problems.

One of these problem elements is carbonate ions. These ions are the chief culprits in the formation of scale, cloudiness and residue.

If all the water's alkalinity is in the harmless bicarbonate form, no scale will develop. If enough of it is in the carbonate form, scale will develop. To avoid formation of carbonates and to keep total alkalinity in the desired bicarbonate form, keep pH level in the recommended range. The ideal level of total alkalinity is from 90 ppm to 150 ppm.

Altering Total Alkalinity Levels—A dilute solution of *sodium bicarbonate,* or baking soda, is used to raise total alkalinity. This solution is made in identical proportions to those used for pH controls: two cups of baking soda to 1 gallon of water. The table on page 145 shows the recommended doses of dilute solution to raise total alkalinity.

Turn on the circulatory system of the spa or hot tub. Pour the prescribed dosage of sodium bicarbonate solution directly into the water. Continue circulating for 30 minutes to ensure good mixing. Then check the pH. This solution may increase pH as high as 8.4. Adjust if necessary.

A dilute solution of *sodium bisulfate,* dry acid, is used to lower total alkalinity. This solution is made in the same manner and proportions as the other solutions mentioned in this chapter. The table on page 145 shows the recommended doses to decrease total alkalinity.

Be careful when using acid solution. Improper use can cause injury and burns to the skin, eyes and clothing.

Turn the circulatory system *off* and allow the water to become motionless. Protecting eyes and body, carefully measure the prescribed dosage of dilute acid solution.

Pour the recommended dosage into the motionless water at its deepest point, being careful not to splash the solution. Do not pour it over a large area. Pour all of the required dilute acid solution into no more than a 12-inch circle.

Turn the circulatory system on. Allow the water to circulate for 30 minutes. Then test the pH. A decrease in pH is usual. Adjust if necessary.

TOTAL DISSOLVED SOLIDS

Total dissolved solids are present in all spas and tubs. However, they're concentrated in areas where high rates of evaporation occur, such as in the warm weather climates of the Southwest. At high levels, such as over 1,500 ppm, total dissolved solids surround bacteria. This prohibits chlorine from working. It can also cause cloudy water and increased foaming.

The variable temperature chart on page 149 indicates proper levels of total alkalinity, pH and calcium hardness at different average water temperatures. The chart assumes that the level of total dissolved solids is in the 500 ppm to 1,500 ppm range.

The best way to keep total dissolved solids in this range is to completely drain and refill the spa or tub every two to three months. Commercial spas should be drained more frequently, at least once a month.

Where do total dissolved solids come from? The water going into the spa or tub usually contains hardness such as calcium and alkalinelike carbonates. It may also contain dissolved organic and inorganic materials such as sulfates or silicates. Salts from residual chlorine, sweat, urine, soluble hair sprays and body lotions add to the total solids. If the unit is outside,

Standard test kits like this one are used to test chlorine level, pH level, calcium hardness and total alkalinity.

wind-blown dirt, leaves, grass clippings and rain-carried pollutants all get into the spa or tub. Particles too small to get trapped by the skimmer or filter dissolve in the water, adding to the concentration.

The effects of evaporation may double or triple the solids content in one year. In Arizona, for example, the evaporation rate is 12 feet per year. In Florida, it is about 6 feet to 8 feet per year. Only the water evaporates. The dissolved solids remain behind and become more and more concentrated as replacement water is added.

A tea kettle illustrates this well. You've seen the white or gray crust that remains after tap water is boiled away. The same thing happens in a pool or spa.

TESTING AND BALANCING WATER

The first part of this chapter discussed the uses of chemicals in water treatment and how to mix them. The next step is to test the water in your own spa or tub, then add the needed chemical solutions in correct proportions to balance the water.

FIVE GOVERNING FACTORS

Water balance in a spa or tub revolves around a theoretical calcium carbonate $(CaCO_3)$ point of saturation. This ideal point is determinated by the interrelationship of five factors:

pH
Total alkalinity
Calcium hardness
Water temperature
Total dissolved solids

Each factor, or any combination, can be altered to achieve balanced water. The point of testing the water is to determine the levels of each and how much it must be altered to bring the water back in balance.

USE A RELIABLE TEST KIT

Valid test data is vital to good water management. Unless you can measure each water-balance factor accurately, it will be almost impossible to balance the water. There's nothing difficult about performing tests for pH, calcium hardness or total alkalinity. A complete test kit should do all of these. Reliable, easy-to-use kits are available from a number of good test-kit manufacturers. A typical test kit is shown at left.

HOW TO DETERMINE AVERAGE TEMPERATURE

Before you can correctly determine the proper levels for pH, calcium hardness and total alkalinity, you'll need to know the average temperature of the spa or tub water. Water temperatures in spas and hot tubs can vary from 70F to 105F (21C to 41C). It's impossible to suggest ideal pH, total alkalinity and calcium hardness levels for the entire temperature range. The best advice is to balance around the average temperature.

Determine average temperature by testing the water when it's at its highest and lowest temperature levels and averaging the two. Example: After heating your spa or tub for use to 104F (40C), you regularly turn off the heater until the next use. Check the temperature of the water before you heat the spa the next time. Let's say the water was 82F (28C), prior to heating. The average water temperature would be the sum of the high and low temperatures, divided by 2, or 82 + 104 = 186 ÷ 2 = 94. So 94F (34C to 35C) would be the average temperature.

Once you determine the average water temperature, record the number for future use. If you heat your spa or tub continuously, check the temperature three or four times during a 24-hour period. The average temperature will be the sum of these temperatures divided by the number of times you checked.

The water should be at its average temperature when you test for water balance. So you may have to cool or heat the water before testing. If you need to cool the water, make sure it circulates through the system for at least one hour after shutting the heater off, or until it reaches the average temperature. This will minimize scale formation within the heater and pipes.

Once the average water temperature has been reached, you can begin testing and balancing the water. It's important to make tests and add chemicals in the correct sequence. The following chemical maintenance guide outlines the procedures for testing and balancing water initially, and on a daily basis.

CHEMICAL MAINTENANCE GUIDE

Initial Maintenance—Read the manufacturer's instructions for your spa or hot tub, as well as the directions for using the pump, bubblers, hydrojets, heater and filter.

If you have a fiberglass spa with an acrylic or gelcoat surface, thoroughly clean it before filling it with water. Wash off dirt and grease with a mild soap and warm water and rinse thoroughly. Gelcoat spas should then be polished. Use a polish recommended by the spa manufacturer. Gelcoat spas require a polish based on *amino-functional fluids*. See page 151. Follow application instructions on the container.

Using a garden hose, fill the spa or tub to the depth recommended by the manufacturer. If you have a wooden tub, do *not* add any chemicals until the wood has swollen to make it watertight.

Tie an old towel around the hose nozzle to act as a crude filter. This also protects the surface of fiberglass spas. If there are high levels of iron or copper present in the water, this is the time to add a sequestering agent to rid

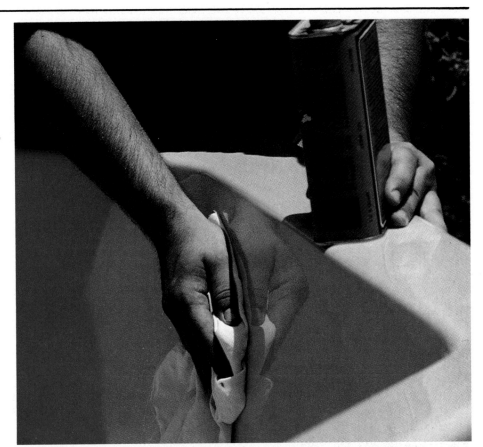

Gelcoat spas should be polished before they're filled with water. Use a gelcoat polish based on amino-functional fluids. The surface will require polishing about every 2 months.

When filling a spa or tub with water, tie an old towel around the hose nozzle. This will help filter the water and protect the finish of gelcoat- or acrylic-surfaced spas.

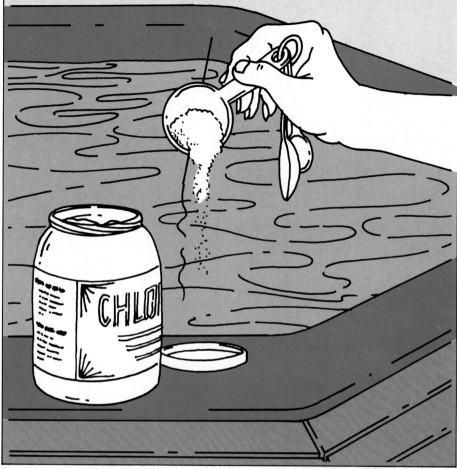

Use a measuring spoon to add exact dosage of granulated chlorine to water. Some brands supply a spoon for this purpose. Do not pour chlorine in or near skimmer.

As a general rule, first adjust total alkalinity and calcium hardness, if needed. Changing these levels will affect pH, so you'll need to retest before adjusting pH level. Next, adjust pH. Adjust chlorine level last.

Add a clarifier to "polish" the water. Clarifiers make tiny particles stick together in larger groups so they are large enough to get trapped in the filter. Use recommended amounts.

Heat the water. Set the thermostat no higher than 104F (40C). Keep the spa or tub covered when not in use. This conserves heat, reduces water and chemical evaporation, and keeps out debris.

The day after you have balanced and sanitized the water and have the support equipment working properly, check the pH, total alkalinity and chlorine level again. Adjust as necessary. After the initial start-up procedure, follow the regular maintenance program described.

REGULAR MAINTENANCE PROGRAM

Balancing The Water—Before you start the process for balancing the spa or tub water, be sure you know exactly how many gallons of water your spa or tub holds. This is essential when it's time to adjust water chemistry.

Determine the average water temperature of your spa or tub, as described on page 142. Record the figure for future use.

Using your test kit, check the pH, total alkalinity and calcium hardness of the water. Record the figures.

Refer to the *variable temperature chart* on page 149 and read instructions on how to use it. On the chart, lightly pencil a straight line connecting the observed total alkalinity level with the observed calcium hardness level, based on tests in previous step.

Find the temperature column in the chart that corresponds to the average temperature of the water and make a note of the observed pH, from step 3, in the instructions.

The ideal pH level for your spa will be indicated at the point where the line drawn in step 4 intersects a pH level in the appropriate temperature column. If tests show the water is balanced, you can then add chlorine to disinfect the water. See "Sanitizing the Water" on page 147.

the water of these metals. Ask a spa or pool dealer where you can get this product.

When the unit is filled to the proper level, turn the heater, pump and filter on. Make sure the system is working properly. If you have problems with any of the components, have the dealer or installer correct them before you proceed any further.

Add chlorine to the water. Use approximately 3/4 to 1 ounce of dry, granulated sodium dichlor chlorine per 500 gallons of water. Do not pour granules near the skimmer. Run the pump and filter for 4 hours to 6 hours, or overnight, until the water clears.

After the water has cleared, test the total alkalinity, calcium hardness, pH level and chlorine level, using a test kit. To test and adjust levels, follow instructions under "Regular Maintenance Program," at right.

If levels need adjusting, make dilute solutions of the needed chemicals. See pages 139-142 for required chemicals and how to mix them.

Decreasing Total Alkalinity (TA) Dilute Acid Solution					
Amount of Dilute Solution	**GALLONS IN SPA OR HOT TUB**				
	200 Gals.	400 Gals.	600 Gals.	800 Gals.	1,000 Gals.
1/4 Cup	5ppm	3ppm	2ppm	1ppm	1ppm
1/2 Cup	11ppm	5ppm	4ppm	3ppm	2ppm
3/4 Cup	16ppm	8ppm	5ppm	4ppm	3ppm
1 Cup	21ppm	11ppm	7ppm	5ppm	4ppm
1 Pint	42ppm	21ppm	14ppm	11ppm	9ppm
1 Quart	84ppm	42ppm	28ppm	21ppm	17ppm
2 Quarts	DON'T	84ppm	57ppm	42ppm	34ppm
3 Quarts	DON'T	DON'T	84ppm	63ppm	52ppm
1 Gallon	DON'T	DON'T	DON'T	84ppm	67ppm

Note: ppm figures represent parts per million increase that will result with that dose.

Increasing Total Alkalinity (TA) Dilute Sodium Bicarbonate Solution					
Amount of Dilute Solution	**GALLONS IN SPA OR HOT TUB**				
	200 Gals.	400 Gals.	600 Gals.	800 Gals.	1,000 Gals.
1/4 Cup	5ppm	3ppm	2ppm	1ppm	1ppm
1/2 Cup	10ppm	5ppm	4ppm	3ppm	2ppm
3/4 Cup	16ppm	8ppm	5ppm	4ppm	3ppm
1 Cup	21ppm	11ppm	7ppm	5ppm	4ppm
1 Pint	42ppm	21ppm	14ppm	11ppm	8ppm
1 Quart	84ppm	42ppm	28ppm	21ppm	17ppm
2 Quarts	DON'T	84ppm	56ppm	42ppm	34ppm
3 Quarts	DON'T	DON'T	84ppm	63ppm	52ppm
1 Gallon	DON'T	DON'T	DON'T	84ppm	67ppm

Note: ppm figures represent parts per million increase that will result with that dose.

If the water isn't balanced, you'll need to adjust the pH level. At the same time, note the calcium hardness and total alkalinity levels from your tests. The bracketed numbers on the chart indicate the ideal range of levels for total alkalinity and calcium hardness. Adjust these levels, if necessary, before making final pH adjustment. Because total alkalinity and calcium hardness affect pH, retest pH if you've adjusted these factors.

Adjusting Total Alkalinity—First determine whether or not you need to raise or lower the total alkalinity of the water. Ideal levels of total alkalinity are between 90 ppm and 150 ppm. If the reading is above 150 ppm, you'll want to lower the total alkalinity using a dilute solution of sodium bisulfate and water. If the total alkalinity is below 90 ppm, you can raise the level with a dilute solution of sodium bicarbonate and water. See page 141 for instructions on making dilute solutions.

Lowering the total alkalinity. Be extra careful when handling acid. Have the dilute solution ready and consult the above table to see how much you'll need to lower the total alkalinity to the proper level.

Turn the circulatory system off and allow the water to become motionless. Protecting the eyes and body, carefully measure the prescribed dosage of dilute acid solution; do not spill or splash.

Pour the recommended dosage into the motionless water at its deepest point. Do not pour over a large area. Pour all of the required dilute acid solution into no more than a 12-inch circle.

Wait 3 minutes to 5 minutes. Turn the circulatory system on. Allow the water to circulate for 30 minutes and then test the pH. A decrease in pH is normal; correct, using the procedure outlined on page 146.

Raising the total alkalinity. Have the dilute solution of sodium bicarbonate and water ready. Consult the above table for the amount of solution needed to raise the total alkalinity to the proper level.

With the circulatory system turned on, pour the prescribed dosage of the sodium-bicarbonate solution directly into the swirling water. Continue circulating for 30 minutes to assure good mixing; then check the pH of the water. This solution has a tendency to increase the pH as high as 8.4. You can correct this when you adjust the pH level.

Adjusting Calcium Hardness—First determine whether you need to raise or lower the level of calcium hardness in the spa or tub water. The ideal levels are between 150 and 450 ppm.

If the reading is below the 150 ppm level, raise the calcium hardness with a dilute solution of calcium chloride and water. See page 141 for directions in making the dilute solution. If the reading is above the 450 ppm level, which is common in areas with hard water, use a sequestering agent or polymer product to remove these

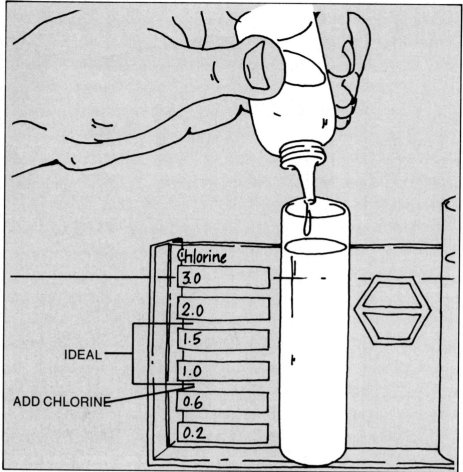

Use test kit to measure chlorine level. Ideal levels are between 1.0 and 1.5 ppm.

Tannins in wood of new hot tub will discolor water for first several months after installation. Though unsightly, water is harmless to tub users.

tized, and ready for use.

Each time you're finished using the unit, superchlorinate the water, following the manufacturer's directions for the amount to use. The amount will be based on the number of gallons the spa or tub holds. When you've added the chlorine, agitate the water for 15 seconds to 30 seconds using the hydrojets or air bubblers. If you have a cover, put it over the spa or tub to slow chlorine evaporation. Check the chlorine level before the next use.

SPECIAL HOT-TUB MAINTENANCE

Although many people think hot tubs require more upkeep than spas, the demands are about the same. What's different is the *type* of maintenance required.

Here are some maintenance tips for owners of cedar and redwood tubs.

INITIAL TREATMENT

During the first few months, water will leach some harmless organic chemicals, including *tannins,* from the wood. These will make the water turn reddish brown. To clear the water in two weeks or less, follow one of these methods:

The simplest approach is to fill and drain the tub frequently. Running the filter two or three hours a day will also help. There's a specially prepared water clarifier that traps tannins in the filter. Check hot-tub suppliers for this device.

Treat wood with a washing solution containing sodium phosphate. Mix about 1 pound of washing solution in a couple of gallons of hot water. Add the solution to the tub and let stand overnight. Drain the tub, then refill it. Wait one week, then repeat the process. Continue treatments until water clears.

Twice a week, for the first two weeks, use a product specially formulated for tub use that contains organic polymers. Remove the hot-tub cover. Turn on the pump. Set the heater thermostat at 90F to 100F (32C to 38C) and leave the air controls turned off. In a pail of water, dilute 1 ounce of the polymer clarifier per 400 gallons of tub water. Pour this slowly into the tub over the total surface area of the water. After adding the polymer product, set time clock or switch to run the filter three to four hours continuously.

The filter may need cleaning during the first two weeks. Check the filter pressure gauge. Clean the filter if water pressure rises over 5 pounds above the normal reading. If your tub
Continued on page 150

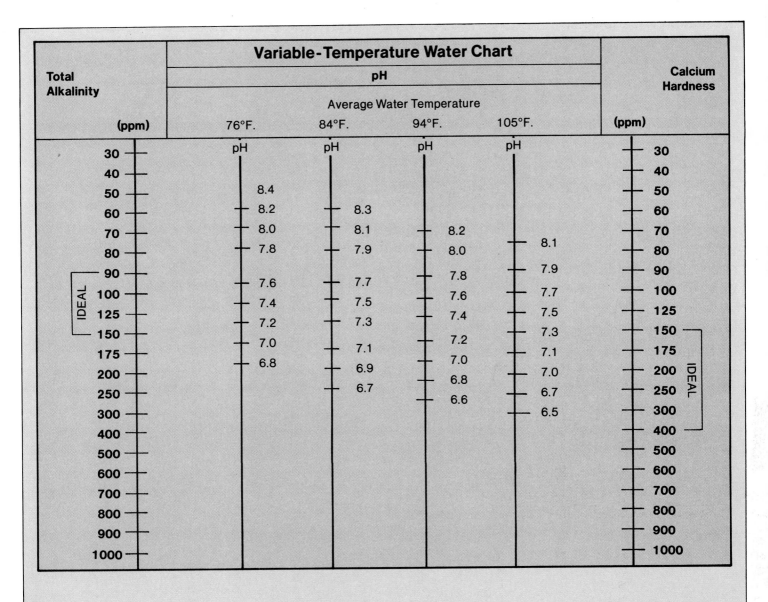

Total Alkalinity	Variable-Temperature Water Chart					Calcium Hardness
	pH					
	Average Water Temperature					
(ppm)	76°F.	84°F.	94°F.	105°F.		(ppm)
	pH	pH	pH	pH		
30						30
40						40
50	8.4					50
60	8.2	8.3				60
70	8.0	8.1	8.2			70
80	7.8	7.9	8.0	8.1		80
90			7.8	7.9		90
100	7.6	7.7	7.6	7.7		100
125	7.4	7.5	7.4	7.5		125
150	7.2	7.3		7.3		150
175	7.0	7.1	7.2	7.1		175
200	6.8	6.9	7.0	7.0		200
250		6.7	6.8	6.7		250
300			6.6	6.5		300
400						400
500						500
600						600
700						700
800						800
900						900
1000						1000

HOW TO USE THIS CHART

This *Variable-Temperature Water Chart* permits the speedy calculation of ideal saturations at four average temperatures. As indicated on page 141, it presumes a level of total dissolved solids of less than 1,500 ppm. It allows for a variation equal to 0.2 pH units up or down a given pH-temperature column.

The chart is reprinted with the permission of Taylor Chemicals.

To use the chart follow these steps:

1. Test spa or tub water for total alkalinity, pH and calcium hardness. Record results.

2. Draw a straight line on the chart connecting the observed total alkalinity with the observed calcium hardness.

3. Choose the appropriate temperature column on the chart. Note the observed pH of the spa water from the test in step 1.

4. Ideal pH of saturation for your test results is the pH indicated by the intersection of the line drawn in step 2 and the appropriate temperature-pH column.

If observed pH is greater than the ideal pH of saturation, undesirable scale-forming potential may exist. If observed pH is less than the ideal pH of saturation in step 4, undesirable corrosive potential may exist.

Any time there's a difference of more than 0.2 pH units between observed pH and ideal pH of saturation, adjustment of one or more of the controlling factors in water balance is indicated.

Here's an example of actual test results from using the chart. The average temperature was 94F (34C to 35C). The pH test (step 1) revealed a pH level of 7.2. Test results were marked in the margin of the chart.

The total alkalinity test gave a reading of 110, so a mark was made between the 100 and 125 levels in the total alkalinity column on the chart.

The calcium hardness test gave a reading of approximately 270, so a mark was made between the 250 and 300 readings in the calcium hardness column of the chart.

Next a line was drawn connecting the two marks. Looking in the appropriate temperature column for this example, 94F (34C to 35C), the line intersected a pH level of 7.0 as the "ideal" level. The pH test, which revealed a pH level of 7.2, indicates a safe margin of 0.2 pH units, above or below the "ideal" level. This shows that the spa water is balanced.

has a cartridge-type filter, soak the filter element in dry dishwashing detergent and water. Thoroughly rinse it with clean water. Sand and DE (diatomaceous earth) filters should be backwashed according to manufacturers' instructions.

Drain the tub after the first two weeks of use. The hot water will have leached out most of the tannin. Cedar tubs should be drained at least twice in the first month.

COMMON PROBLEMS WITH HOT TUBS

Here are repair solutions for some of the main service problems with wooden hot tubs.

LEAK IN THE CROZE

Causes—Over-chlorination, no air to bottom of tub, deck too tight at top, lower band not opposite croze.

Prevention—Make sure the lower band is opposite the croze. Assure air flow under the tub. Allow at least 1/2-inch clearance around the tub from deck to allow for swelling when the tub is filled with water.

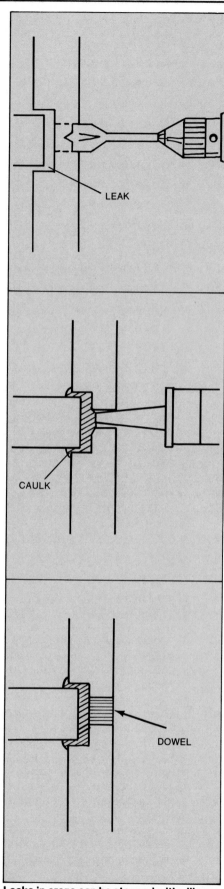

Leaks in croze can be stopped with silicone caulk. Drill 1/2-inch hole in stave opposite leak, inject caulk in croze void and patch hole with wood dowel.

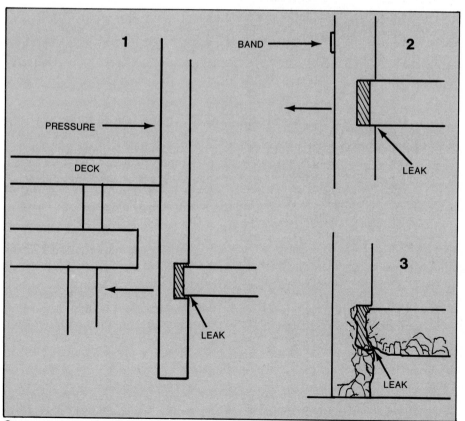

Common causes of leaks in tub croze are: 1. Decking too tight around top of tub. 2. Lower band or hoop not aligned with croze. 3. Wood deterioration caused by over-chlorination or poor air circulation under tub.

Repair—For this process, you'll need a drill with a 1/2-inch wood bit, caulking gun, silicone caulk and a short length of 1/2-inch dowel. Dowel should be of the same wood as the tub staves, if possible.

First drain the tub. Then drill a 1/2-inch hole through the outside of the stave, opposite the croze joint where the leak occurs. Drill slowly. You will feel the drill bit enter the void of the croze joint. Next, use the caulking gun to pump caulk into the croze joint. The caulk will travel two or three staves and stop the leak. Plug the hole in stave with a dowel.

LEAK IN STAVES

Cause—Tub left without water too long.

Repair—Where leak occurs, pack outside joints between staves with absorbent cotton cord or twine. Mop strings work well. Use a putty knife or chisel to stuff the cord tightly into the joints. If the cord is kept tightly packed, the staves will soon swell back into shape.

If staves are unevenly assembled, or a filler or caulk was used, you may have to take the tub apart and reassemble it to align the staves. Although some old-timers recommend using sawdust or flax seed to stop leaks, don't. Even if they seem to work, they're only a temporary solution.

WOOD DISINTEGRATING INSIDE TUB

Cause—Over-chlorination has deteriorated soft part of wood. Chlorine breaks down wood *lignin,* the substance that binds wood cells together.

Prevention—Apply chlorine in recommended doses. Chlorinate only when chlorine level falls below safe margins. See page 149.

Repair—Empty tub. Sand damaged surface down to sound wood. Use waterproof sandpaper over a sanding block. If damage is severe, rough sand with 120-grit paper and smooth out with a finer grade paper. Rinse out tub. Any remaining damaged wood will eventually peel off and get trapped in the filter.

GROWTH ON INSIDE OR OUTSIDE OF TUB

Cause—Improper water chemistry.
Cure—Check water balance and correct, if necessary. Make sure you're

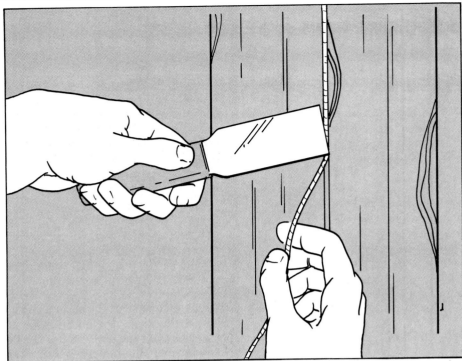

To fix leaks between staves, use a chisel or putty knife to stuff cracks with cotton cord or twine.

using the proper amount of chlorine. If the growth persists, do not rely on superchlorination. Chlorine will not kill all growths. Take a sample of the growth to the health department or a testing laboratory for identification. To find the proper lab, look in the Yellow Pages under "Laboratories, Testing." Find out the safest and best way to kill the growth.

MAINTAINING A GELCOAT SPA SURFACE

The surface of a spa is constantly assaulted by harsh environmental enemies. Wind, rain, sunshine, smog, chemicals and hot water are all damaging. On a gelcoat spa, they cause rust, pitting, corrosion, oxidation, color fading and loss of surface gloss. For years, paraffin-based waxes were the only solution.

Modern technology has produced new coatings, called *amino-functional fluids* or commonly, *hard-surface sealants.*

Wax-based products are soft-surface coatings without bonding capabilities. Amino-functional coatings actually bond chemically to the spa surface and become part of the finish. A paraffin-based coating will break down quickly under intense heat, abrasion and environmental exposure. Sometimes this occurs in just a few days.

Acrylic spas can be patched using ordinary auto-body filler, available at auto-supply stores. Spa manufacturers provide repair kits that include instructions and acrylic touch-up paints that match spa colors. Paints are applied with an air brush, as shown here. Air brushes are available at art-supply stores.

WHEN YOU HAVE A COMPLAINT

The best way to avoid disappointment with your spa or tub is to buy a quality product from a reputable dealer. But even the most careful and knowledgeable buyers occasionally find themselves with a real problem on their hands.

If you have a problem, where can you go for help? First contact the dealer and work with him to resolve the problem. If the problem is with the spa or tub construction, or with the support equipment, contact the manufacturer. If you still can't get the problem resolved, here are a few suggestions:

NATIONAL SPA AND POOL INSTITUTE

The National Spa and Pool Institute (NSPI) currently represents approximately 3,000 pool, spa and hot-tub manufacturers and retailers. Although buying a spa or tub from an NSPI member won't guarantee perfection, the dealer will be more receptive to your complaints or comments.

The NSPI has formed an ethics committee that reviews these matters and offers help to consumers. Complaints must be in writing. Send to National Spa and Pool Institute, 2111 Eisenhower Ave., Alexandria, VA 22314. Telephone 703/838-0083.

The NSPI also has a number of publications for spa, hot tub and swimming pool owners, as well as for spa and pool dealers and installers. Included are brochures on safe use of spas, hot tubs and pools, operation and maintenance tips, energy saving ideas, planning tips and more. A publications list is available upon request.

BETTER BUSINESS BUREAUS

Better Business Bureaus in most cities have three requirements for handling complaints: The complaint must be received on the Bureau's pre-printed forms. The business or consumer must reside in the county where the bureau is located. Two first-class stamps must be enclosed with the complaint form.

Look in the phone book for the address of the nearest Better Business Bureau office. Some offices have a complaint line. If so, when you call, you'll hear a recorded message requesting your name and address. A complaint form will be sent to you. If there is no complaint line, write for a complaint form.

When the complaint is received, a copy of it is sent to the business in question. The business is asked to respond directly to you.

A follow-up or status card is included with the original complaint card you received. You should keep it for 30 days. If the business has not responded within that time, send the follow-up card back to the Better Business Bureau. They'll contact the business directly. If there's still no satisfactory response, the Better Business Bureau will refer you to a small-claims court.

CONTRACTORS' STATE LICENSE BOARD

Most states in the United States have a Contractors' State License Board that is a division of the State Department of Consumer Affairs. This agency is in charge of statewide licensing of contractors and has the power to revoke a contractor's license.

If you have a complaint about any aspect of contracted work, write the Contractors' State License Board. Look in the white pages of the telephone book for the address of the nearest office.

Once a complaint has been received in writing, it's reviewed by a complaint board. An investigator is assigned to the case. If the board determines the contractor is at fault, disciplinary action is taken through the State Attorney General's office. This can result in suspension or revocation of the contractor's license.

Prior to reinstatement, the contractor may have to post a bond for the purpose of settling previous claims made by consumers, including yours.

SPA AND HOT-TUB SAFETY

Spas and hot tubs are enjoyable, healthful and safe if used properly. Here are some basic rules:

CHECK FIRST

Persons suffering from heart disease, diabetes or high or low blood pressure should check with their doctor *before* using a spa or hot tub. A person with an open wound or acute swelling from a sprain should *not* soak in a spa or hot tub.

PREGNANCY AND SOAKING

Medical authorities disagree on the effects soaking in a spa or tub has on

Small children cannot withstand the same water temperatures as adults. Physicians generally recommend 95F to 98F (35C to 37C) water temperature for children under five. Limit soaking time to 12 minutes or less.

pregnant women. Studies have shown, though, that spa and tub use can result in hyperthermia, or overheating of the body. In pregnant women, this condition can decrease blood flow to the fetus. If the pregnancy is complicated, this can threaten the infant.

Another potential problem with spa and hot-tub use is the spread of organisms that may cause vaginal infections.

Some medical researchers believe that spa and tub soaking may have other harmful effects on pregnant women, but their research has not been conclusive.

Many doctors advise their patients not to use spa or tubs at all. Others may recommend safe water temperatures and soaking periods. In all cases, a pregnant woman should consult her physician before using a spa or hot tub.

ALCOHOL AND MEDICATIONS

Beware of drinking while using a spa or hot tub. Alcohol and hot water can form a deadly combination.

Hot water increases your blood flow. Consequently, alcohol in the bloodstream will reach its destination much faster than under normal circumstances. Your usual quota of alcohol may leave you much more intoxicated than expected.

Medical authorities suggest that you not mix alcoholic beverages and spa use at all. They point out that a spa or hot tub offers natural relaxation so there should be no need for a sedating drug like alcohol.

People using medication of any sort should check with their doctor before using a spa or tub. *Do not* use a spa or tub while under the influence of alcohol, anticoagulants, antihistamines, vasoconstrictors, vasodilators, stimulants, hypnotics, narcotics or tranquilizers.

WATER TEMPERATURE

Many doctors recommend that spas and hot tubs be heated to no more than 104F (40C) for home use. For children under 5 years old, a water temperature of 95F to 98F (35C to 37C) is suggested. Anyone experiencing flushing, dizziness or a headache while in the spa should get out as quickly as possible.

The water temperature should be checked regularly. If the temperature is 104F (40C)—soaking should be limited to no more than 12 minutes.

LONG HAIR

People with long hair, especially children, should avoid putting their head underwater near the drain. The suction can be powerful enough to pull hair into the drain. It then becomes entangled and is difficult to pull free. Several spa and tub users have drowned as a result of getting their hair caught in the drain.

As an additional precaution, bathers with long hair should either tie it back or wear a bathing cap. Also, some spas and tubs have safer drains than others. When buying a spa or tub, ask the dealer if drain suction is a potential danger.

POST THE SAFETY RULES

The National Spa and Pool Institute recently introduced a *Hot-Water Safety Sign.* It reads as follows:
• Pregnant women and persons suffering from heart disease, diabetes, high or low blood pressure should not enter the spa/hot tub without prior medical consultation and permission from their doctor.
• Do not use the spa/hot tub while under the influence of alcohol, anticoagulants, antihistamines, vasoconstrictors, vasodilators, stimulants, hypnotics, narcotics or tranquilizers.
• Check spa/hot tub water temperature before use. Maximum safe temperature is 104F (40C).
• Do not use alone.
• Unsupervised use by children is prohibited.
• Enter and exit slowly.
• Observe reasonable time limits to avoid nausea, dizziness and fainting.
• Keep all breakable objects out of the area.
• Emergency telephone numbers for police, fire and rescue squad should be posted at the nearest telephone.

The sign is predrilled for easy installation and is made of long-lasting, weather-resistant plastic. The sign should be posted in full view of anyone using the spa or tub.

The safety sign can be ordered from the NSPI, 2111 Eisenhower Ave., Alexandria, VA 22314. The telephone number is 703/838-0083. Write or call for price and availability.

Index

Temperature

°F	°C	°F	°C	°F	°C
−26	−32	19	−7	64	18
−24	−31	21	−6	66	19
−22	−30	23	−5	68	20
−20	−29	25	−4	70	21
−18	−28	27	−3	72	22
−17	−27	28	−2	73	23
−15	−26	30	−1	75	24
−13	−25	32	0	77	25
−11	−24	34	1	79	26
−9	−23	36	2	81	27
−8	−22	37	3	82	28
−6	−21	39	4	84	29
−4	−20	41	5	86	30
−2	−19	43	6	88	31
0	−18	45	7	90	32
1	−17	46	8	91	33
3	−16	48	9	93	34
5	−15	50	10	95	35
7	−14	52	11	97	36
9	−13	54	12	99	12
10	−12	55	13	100	38
12	−11	57	14	102	39
14	−10	59	15	104	40
16	−9	61	16	106	41
18	8	63	17	108	42

Conversion Formula:
$$°F = 32 + (°C \times 1.8)$$
$$°C = (°F - 32) \times .56$$

Metric Chart

Comparison to Metric Measure

When You Know	Symbol	Multiply By	To Find	Symbol
teaspoons	tsp.	5.00	milliliters	ml
tablespoons	tbsp.	15.00	milliliters	ml
fluid ounces	fl. oz.	30.00	milliliters	ml
cups	c.	0.24	liters	l
pints	pt.	0.47	liters	l
quarts	qt.	0.95	liters	l
gallons	gal.	3.8	liters	l
ounces	oz.	28.00	grams	g
pounds	lb.	0.45	kilograms	kg
inches	in.	2.54	centimeters	cm
feet	ft.	30.00	centimeters	cm

Acknowledgments

We would like to thank the following people and firms for their valuable assistance:

Beachport Spas, Tustin, CA
Mike Bergin, Piedmont, CA
California Cooperage, San Luis Obispo, CA
John Cannaley, Campbell Design Associates, Tucson, AZ
Consolidated Pool Mart Inc., Tucson, AZ
Faye Coupe and Jorian Clair, Pool & Spa News, Los Angeles, CA
Mike Grisham, FAFCO Inc., Menlo Park, CA
Hydrotech, Marietta, GA
International Spa and Tub Institute, Santa Ana, CA
Skip Lane, Barrel Builders, St. Helena, CA
National Spa and Pool Institute, Washington, D.C.
Warren Nicholson and Don Wangerman, Don's Pool Center, Napa, CA
Beth Parker, Spa and Sauna Trade Journal, Santa Ana, CA
John S. Ryan, M.D., University of California Medical Center, Irvine, CA
Satori Spas, Berkeley, CA
Taylor Chemicals, Baltimore, MD
Teledyne Laars, North Hollywood, CA

We would like to thank the following landscape architects, designers and companies whose spa and hot-tub designs appeared in this book:

Batter-Kay, Solana Beach, CA: 1, 40 top right, 69 bottom.
Edward Carson Beall, AIA, Torrance, CA: 7, 38 top, 50, 51 top.
Mark Berry, Landscape Architect, Pasadena, CA: 157.
John Blanton, Manhattan Beach, CA: 33 top.
California Cooperage, San Luis Obispo, CA: 12 bottom right, 14 top, 53, 56 bottom, 66 center, 70 bottom right, 73 center, 99, 134, 135.
California Pools & Spas, El Monte, CA: 12 top right, 64 top.
Catalina Spas & Hot Tubs, Tucson, AZ: 73 bottom left.
William Dorich, Los Angeles, CA: Cover, 92 left.
Robert W. Dvorak, Tucson, AZ: 11.
Emerald Pools, Carson, CA: 8, 32 bottom, 36 top, 37 right, 39 bottom, 47 bottom, 48 bottom, 56 top, 138.
Eriksson, Peters and Thoms, ASLA, Pasadena, CA: 28, 31, 39 top right, 68 bottom, 69 top right, 157.
FM Landscaping Inc., Tucson, AZ: 47 top.
Ray Forsum, San Juan Capastrano, CA: 58.
Galper/Baldon & Associates, Landscape Architects, Venice, CA: 39 top left, 48 left, 52, 62 top right, 64 left, 65, 67 bottom, 68 top, 71 top.
Bob Gervassoni, Santa Barbara, CA: 63 bottom, back cover.
May Hagman, Malibu, CA: 34.
Jorgen Hansen, Tucson, AZ: 35.
Gary Humecke, Malibu Spa and Hot Tub, Malibu, CA: 6 bottom, 57 left, 72 top.
Nick Kirov, Emerald Pools, Carson, CA: 8 top.
Tom Marsee, Emerald Pools, Carson, CA: 56 top.
Steve Martino & Associates, Landscape Architects, Phoenix, AZ: 71 bottom left, 73 bottom right.
Jim O'Brien, San Juan Capastrano, CA: 58, 155.
Ken Paulsen, Landscape Architect, Thousand Oaks, CA: 5, 33 bottom left, 61, bottom left, 63 top, 64 bottom right, back cover.
Reed & Reed, Landscape Architects, Beverly Hills, CA: 9 top.
Alan Ross, Landscape Architect, Santa Monica, CA: 30, 49, 73 top.
Jack M Smith, Landscape Architect, Los Angeles, CA: 69 top left.
Gilbert A. Staynor, Los Angeles, CA: 46.
Joseph L. Stecker, Hallmark Pools, Rolling Meadows, IL: 13 right.
Gary Stone, Stone-Fischer & Associates, Del Mar, CA: 55.
Mark Sutter, AIA, Encino, CA: 9 bottom, 12 top right and bottom left, 54, 62 bottom, 72 bottom.
Dennis Taylor, Peridian Group, Irvine, CA: 36 bottom.
Gregg Toland, Landscape Architect, Los Angeles, CA: 2, 59.
Robert Winship, Palos Verdes Pools, Redondo Beach, CA: 62 center.
Ken Wormholdt, Landscape Architect, Pasadena, CA: 61 right.
Walt Young, Landscape Architect, Los Angeles, CA: 4, 12 top left.

Special thanks to our technical consultants for their many contributions to this book:

Bernard Burba, Baja Industries, Tucson, AZ
Leon LaSalle and Ralph Raub, Catalina Spas and Hot Tubs, Tucson, AZ
Andy Vasquez, Spa Parts & Accessories, Westminister, CA

Photography

Major photography by:

Richard Fish
Leland Lee
Tim Fuller
James Brett

Additional photography by:

Friend & Denny Productions
Roland Dare
Steve Martino

Other photos furnished courtesy of:

Baja Industries, Tucson, AZ
California Cooperage, San Luis Obispo, CA
Campbell Design Associates, Tucson, AZ
Emerald Pools, Tustin, CA
Hallmark Pools, Rolling Meadows, IL
Sta-Rite Industries, Delavan, WI

Illustrations:

Major illustrations by Paul Fitzgerald
Additional illustrations by Edith Allgood